Small Craft Plans
15 Complete Designs for Dinghies & Tenders

From the boards of the

Benford Design Group
P.O. Box 447
605 Talbot St.
St. Michaels, MD 21663

Phone: 301-745-3235
Fax: 301-745-9743

Published by:

P.O. Box 447

St. Michaels, MD 21663

Phone: 301-745-3750

Fax: 301-745-9743

Color photos of the 8′ Portland Yawlboat and 16′ Sailing Tender on the covers were generously supplied by Pacific Yachting Magazine.

By the same author:

CRUISING BOATS, SAIL & POWER, 4 editions in 1968, 1969, 1970, & 1971. Catalog of designs and article reprints.

PRACTICAL FERRO-CEMENT BOATBUILD-ING, with Herman Husen, 3 editions in 1970, 1971, and 1972. Best selling construction handbook, a how-to on building in ferro-cement.

DESIGNS & SERVICES, 5 editions, 1971, 1972, 1987, 1988, & 1990. Catalog of plans and services of our firm.

BOATBUILDING & DESIGN FORUM, a monthly newsletter with more information on ferro-cement boatbuilding, 1973.

THE BENFORD 30, 3 editions in 1975, 1976, & 1977. An exposition on the virtues of this design and general philosophy of choosing a cruising boat.

CRUISING DESIGNS, 2 editions in 1975, & 1976. A catalog of plans and services and information about boats & equipment.

CRUISING YACHTS, 1983 hardcover book with a selection of Benford designs covered in detail, including several complete sets of plans and a lot of information about the boats and how they came to be. 8 pages of color photos.

SMALL CRAFT PLANS, 1990 book with 15 sets of full plans for 7′-3" to 18′ dinghies and tenders.

SMALL SHIPS, 1990 book with Benford designs for tugs, freighters (like the Florida Bay Coaster), ferries and excursion boats. 10 pages of color photos.

DESIGN DEVELOPMENT OF A 40m SAILING YACHT, Technical paper presented to the Society of Naval Architects & Marine Engineers, at the 5th (1981) Chesapeake Sailing Yacht Symposium, and in the bound transactions of that meeting.

Table of Contents

How to Use This Book

We have tried to reproduce the plans in this book accurately, in a reduced scale, from the original drawings. In most cases, the drawings are printed at one-half of the original size. The exceptions are page 7 at one-third and pages 6, 9, 74, and 76 at one-quarter of the original scale.

Thus, using an appropriately reduced scale on an architect's scale will permit scaling general measurements off the plans.

I would still recommend lofting full size, and creating the other dimensioning needed off the lofting and dimensions noted on the drawings, rather than trying to work off the small scale drawings. The extra time spent doing the lofting will be saved several times over during the course of building. It will also give you a better chance of doing a first rate job of building a boat we both can be proud of.

I will look forward to seeing photos of boats built from these plans. These photos, along with comments on how the boats worked out for you, will be of great assistance to us in doing updated editions of this book.

Introduction

Small craft are an ever present part of our boating world, whether as pleasure boats on their own or serving as a tender to a larger boat. I've had the pleasure of designing a number of small craft over the last 28 years in this business. Some of the ones I think are worthy of interest are included in this book. I hope you will find them of interest too, and have an opportunity to enjoy using them.

Others whose drawing talents have contributed to these drawings are Peter Dunsford (PAD), Brian Harris (BAH), Jon Stivers (JSS), Bruce Williams (BEMW), Jeff Patterson (JRP), and Tatsuaki Suzuki (chop mark). Many thanks to them for their help.

For several of the designs in this book, we have drawn the lines full size for use in mold frame building. The designs available that way are the 8′ Portland Yawl-boat (design number 148), the 8 1/2′ Dinghy (#164), the 11′ Oregon Peapod (157), and the 11′ Dinghy (#149). Through 1991, we will make these available for $50 each, plus another $20 if we have to airmail overseas. After 1991, check with us to see what's the current price.

The plans printed here are for the use of people wanting to build one boat for themselves. Professional builders wanting to offer any of them as stock boats should contact us regarding royalties for production boats and for details on how we can be of assistance in marketing them.

Jay R. Benford
St. Michaels, Maryland
August 1990

About The Author:

Jay R. Benford was taken sailing before he could walk, by parents unconcerned about the impressions being made on the youth. He was several years old before he determined that this was not perfectly normal procedure on the part of his parents. By then, of course, it was too late for he had become hooked on cruising. His school teachers' pointed remarks about the lack of variety on his book reports (always nautical books) seem to have been of no concern to him. His two years at the University of Michigan led to a much better knowledge of the location of the nautical sections of the libraries than the locations of his classrooms.

He says the best parts of his education were his apprenticeship with John Atkin and the subsequent jobs with a number of boatbuilding firms. After seven years of working for others, he opened his own yacht design office full time in the spring of 1969. Shortly thereafter he got a series of instructive lessons from his accountant in the use of red ink. His recent design work varies from small craft to a 40 meter (131′) ketch, and when not off cruising, he can be found in his St. Michaels, MD, office working on one of his dozen or so current design projects.

Chapter 1
7'-3" Dinghy

Some years ago I was approached by the shop teacher at the Friday Harbor High School about helping with a boatbuilding program at the school. They were looking at building a boat somewhat larger than this, and a lot more complicated. This design was done to give the students something that would go together quickly, and not be beyond the skills that one might assume they'd picked up in the woodworking program.

This meant that complicated bevels and fits were to be avoided and simplicity was to be emphasized. The resulting design has a virtually constant bevel cut for the chine, so this can be run off on a table saw.

The materials were chosen to be readily available from a normal lumberyard's stock. Primarily they are clear fir and a couple of sheets of 1/4" plywood.

Alternatively, she could be done with the stitch and glue technique at the chines, and epoxy sealed and sheathed with a protective layer of cloth set in epoxy.

This sort of boat does best if kept light, so she is easily lifted aboard or onto a cartop for transporting. Keep the towing eye low, as shown, and be sure to fit the skeg shown for best results towing her.

If a sailing rig was wanted, something like that shown on the 8' Portland Yawlboat would work, using her rudder and daggerboard details too.

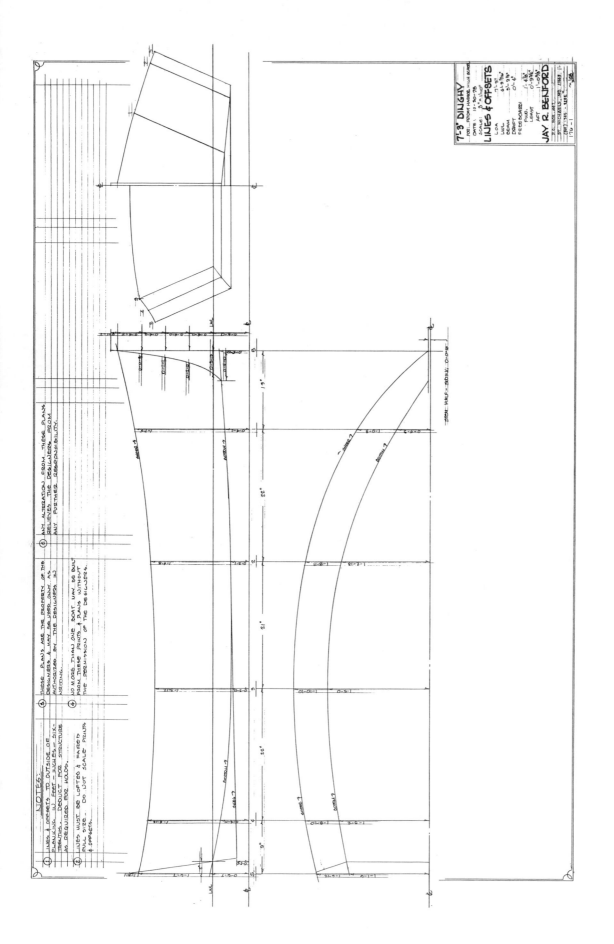

'7'-3" DINGHY
FOR: FRIDAY HARBOR HIGH SCHOOL
DATE: 11-8-78
SCALE: 1½"=1'-0" & AS NOTED
CONST. & OUTFIT

LOA	7'-3"
LWL	6'-9¾"
BEAM	3'-9¾"
DRAFT	0'-4"
FREEBOARDS:	
FWD.	1'-4½"
LEAST	0'-9¾"
AFT	1'-0¾"

JAY R. BENFORD
ST. MICHAELS, MD. 21663
P.O. BOX 447
(301) 745 - 3235
1/W-2

CONSTRUCTION SEQUENCE:

1. LOFT FULL SIZE. DEDUCT FOR PLANKING & FRAMING TO GET MOLD FRAME SIZES.

2. LAYOUT & CUT MOLD FRAMES. NOTCH FOR CHINE & SEAT RISER — BEVEL TO FIT PLANKING.

3. LAYOUT & CUT STEM TO SHAPE. BEVEL TO FIT PLANKING AS SHOWN & NOTCH FOR CHINES.

4. LAYOUT TRANSOM SHAPE & FRAMING. CUT ALL OVERSIZE TO ALLOW FOR REQUIRED BEVELS — BEVEL AS REQUIRED.

5. SET UP MOLDS, STEM, & TRANSOM. CHECK FOR ALIGNMENT, SPACING & BE SURE ALL ARE SQUARE TO REFERENCE PLANE.

6. INSTALL CHINES & THWART RISERS. BEVEL OFF CHINES FOR BOTTOM PLANKING.

7. PUT ON BOTTOM PLANKING. FASTEN TO CHINES, STEM, & TRANSOM FRAME. TRIM OFF FLUSH WITH CHINES & TRANSOM.

8. PUT ON SIDE PLANKING — TRIM OFF FLUSH WITH BOTTOM, STEM, & TRANSOM.

9. INSTALL GUNWALES & TRIM OFF PLANKING AT SHEER.

10. INSTALL SKEG.

11. APPLY BRASS STEM GUARD — MAY BE EXTENDED ALONG BOTTOM & SKEG — UP ONTO TRANSOM.

12. INSTALL MIDDLE THWART.

13. SAND & PREPARE FOR PAINTING. FILL OVER HEADS OF FASTENINGS — RADIUS SHARP CORNERS AT CHINE & TRANSOM — SEAL ALL EXPOSED EDGE & END GRAIN — PAINT.

14. REMOVE FROM MOLDS, & FIT FORE & AFT THWARTS, KNEES AT TRANSOM & BREASTHOOK & OARLOCK PADS AS REQUIRED.

15. REPEAT STEP 13 ON INTERIOR.

16. INSTALL OARLOCKS.

17. LAUNCH & ROW . . . .

NOTE:

ALL FIR. TO BE CLEAR V.G. — ALL PLYWOOD MARINE OR EXTERIOR GRADE — ALL PAYING SURFACES TO BE GLUED AS WELL AS MECHANICALLY FASTENED. GLUE TO BE RESORCINAL OR EPOXY.

SCANTLINGS:

1. STEM: SIDED 1½" FIR

2. CHINES, THWART RISERS & GUNWALES: ¾" x 1½" FIR — BEVELED AS SHOWN.

3. TRANSOM FRAME: 1½" x ¾" FIR.

4. TRANSOM: ¼" PLYWOOD

5. PLANKING: ¼" PLYWOOD

6. SKEG: SIDED ¾" FIR

7. STEM GUARD: ¾" BRASS HALF-OVAL

8. THWARTS: ¼" PLYWOOD ON ¾" x 1½" FIR FRAMES

9. BREASTHOOK & QUARTER KNEES: ¾" APPLE OR FIR

10. ROWLOCK SOCKETS: PERKO FIG. 832 MOUNTED ON ¾" x 1½" x ¼" PAD & THRU-BOLTED TO GUNWALE

11. TOWING EYE: WILCOX-CRITTENDEN SHOULDER EYE-BOLT FIG. 2221 ¼" x 4"

12. BEACHING RUNNERS: (OPTIONAL) ⅜" x ¾" STRIPS WITH HALF-OVAL OVER. ¾" BRASS. ADD ¾" x 2¼" ON ℄ FULL LENGTH ALSO.

INBOARD PROFILE:

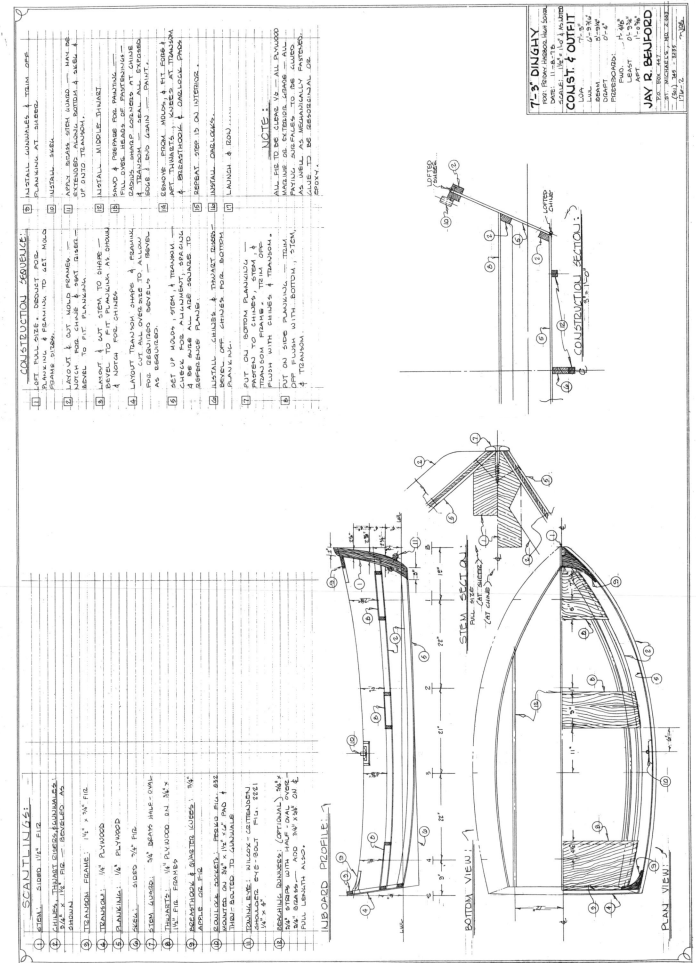

CONSTRUCTION SECTION: 3" = 1'-0"

STEM SECT'N: FULL SIZE

BOTTOM VIEW:

PLAN VIEW:

Chapter 2
7 1/2′ Dinghy

This boat was designed while friends were in the business of building Benford 30's in fiberglass. It looked to be a good size to carry on her aft deck, and I liked her shape.

They built a plug out of plywood, and commented that the narrow double chine panel at the bow was a bit difficult to twist in place, but otherwise she went together easily.

Then, they laid up a mold on the plug. However, they either forgot about the necessity for using some mold release agent or didn't get it uniformly over the boat. About this time, I think that they began to realize thay they were putting in a lot more time doing nice detail work on the B30's than they had put in their estimates when they signed the contracts. So,

this dinghy project was abandoned while they concentrated on turning out several nicely done B30's. They never got back to it, so I can only speculate that I think she'd be a good little tender.

I'd build her of 1/4" plywood, or 3/16" if a really light version was wanted. Scantlings like the 7′-3" dinghy would work. If a sailing rig was wanted, I'd use the one off the 8′ Portland Yawlboat, using the rudder and daggerboard details too.

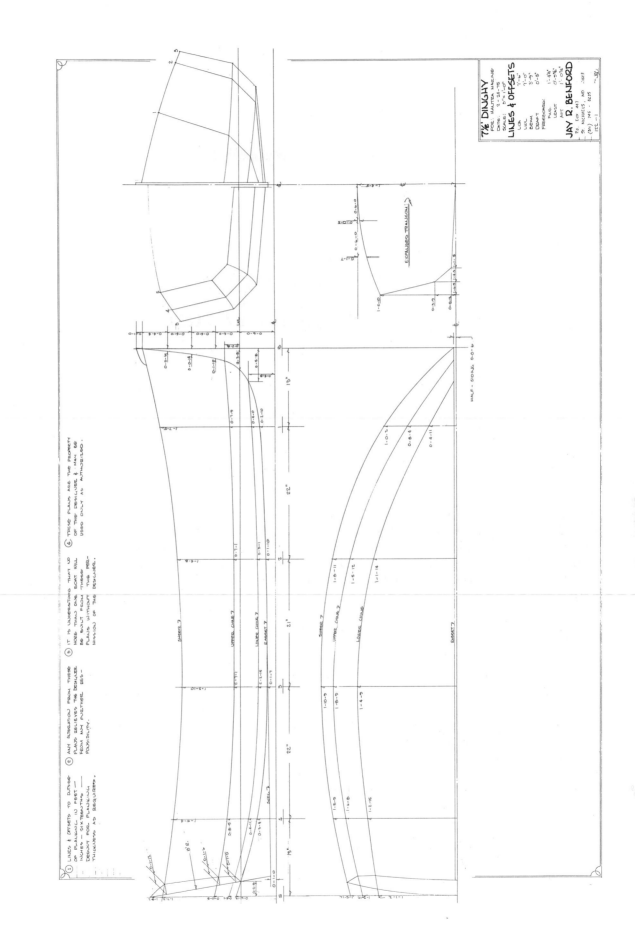

Chapter 3
8′ D.E. Dinghy

This design was commissioned by a builder wanting to do a little boat that was a bit different than the usual run of dinghies. He had a set of lines for a larger dinghy he'd found in a very old book and asked me to scale it to eight feet, so he could build a plug and mold for the boats.

As so often happens when trying to work from a very small print in a book, the published drawings were considerably out of fair. The end result was a lot of refairing work to create a boat with a similar character.

Quite a few boats were molded to this design and I've seen a number of them on my cruises in the Pacific Northwest. They proved to be easily rowed, and I felt they were a success that way. However, due to their narrow beam, they had limited carrying capacity and stability.

I believe that a larger version, say a 50% enlargement to 12′ x 4 1/2′, would be a much more useful boat and not have the limitations the smaller one had. Following this line of thinking is what led to the creation of the 11′ Oregon Peapod, shown later in this book. Using the scantlings and rig from the 11-footer should work well for a 12′ version of this 8′ double ender.

Normally, I am considerably less than enthusiastic about scaling designs from one size to another. This is due to the structural and performance changes that occur at non-linear relationships. However, this exception should work out if my scantling suggestions are followed.

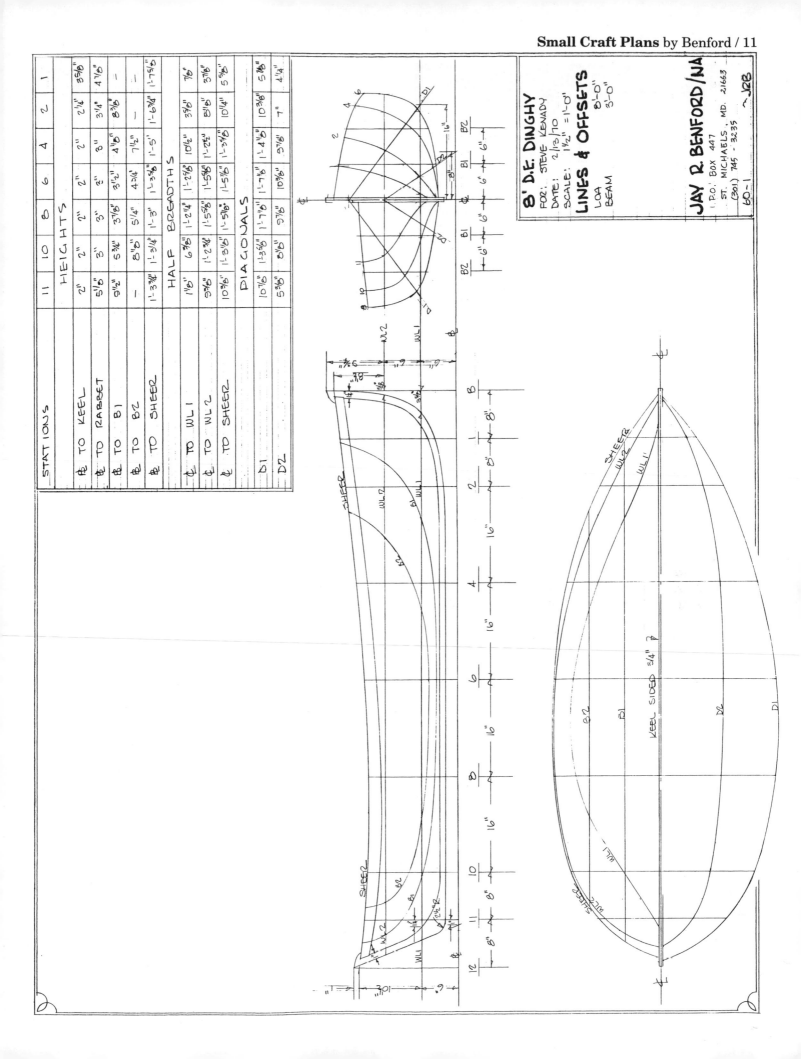

8' D.E. DINGHY
FOR: STEVE KENADY
DATE: 2/13/10
SCALE: 1½" = 1'-0"

LINES & OFFSETS
LOA 8'-0"
BEAM 3'-0"

JAY R. BENFORD/NA
P.O. BOX 447
ST. MICHAELS, MD. 21663
(301) 745 - 3235
60-1

STATIONS	11	10	8	6	4	2	1
HEIGHTS							
℄ TO KEEL	2"	2"	2"	2"	2"	2⅛"	3⅝"
℄ TO RABBET	5⅛"	3"	3"	2"	3¼"	3¼"	4⅞"
℄ TO B1	9½"	5¾"	5⅜"	3⅛"	4⅛"	8⅝"	—
℄ TO B2	—	8½"	5¼"	4¾"	7½"	—	—
℄ TO SHEER	1-3¾"	1-3¼"	1-3"	1-3⅝"	1-5"	1-6¾"	1-7⅝"
HALF BREADTHS							
℄ TO WL1	1⅛"	6⅞"	1-2¼"	10½"	3⅜"	7⅛"	—
℄ TO WL2	9⅝"	1-2½"	1-5⅝"	1-2½"	8⅛"	5⅞"	—
℄ TO SHEER	10⅞"	1-3⅝"	1-5⅛"	1-5⅝"	1-4⅜"	10¼"	5⅝"
DIAGONALS							
D1	10⅞"	1-3⅝"	1-5⅛"	1-4⅜"	10⅜"	7"	4¼"
D2	5⅜"	8⅝"					

KEEL SIDED ¾"

Don Macey's cold-molded 8' Portland Yawlboat (above) nearing completion and Mike Kiefer's traditional lapstrake version (below) ready for service.

Both show nice detailing. Photos courtesy of the builders.

Chapter 4
8′ Portland Yawlboat

The traditional yawlboat is a hard working boat, carried on the stern davits of a larger working vessel. They have sweet shapes to be easily driven and as was befitting the pride of workmanship that went into their construction.

This latter day version is much lighter and smaller in size. She will make a splendid small tender for a larger yacht and a fun small sailing dinghy for kids of all ages. She is light enough to be carried on cartop racks or hung off the stern of a modest size cruiser, or lifted aboard and carried on deck.

Her beamy shape gives her good stability. She will row, tow, and sail well. The skeg aft provides directional stability while rowing or towing. The slot designed into her skeg is there to provide a handhold which will make her easy to lift.

An optional oarlock aft, on the port quarter, will facilitate sculling. She has two oarlock positions on the gunwales. Depending on how she's loaded, the person rowing can sit amidships or forward. Or, two sets of oars can be used for towing operations or training the crew.

For some time, I've thought about designing a version of this boat with another strake of planking, three or four inches in depth, added at the sheer. This would greatly increase her carrying capacity and usefulness as a tender.

Construction alternatives that are practical, beyond those shown on the drawings in this chapter, are Airex-cored fiberglass (see 11′ Oregon Peapod for an example) and cedar strips sheathed in fiberglass cloth and epoxy resin.

The lovely example of this design shown on the front cover of this book was built by John and James Guzzwell. She is used as tender to the cold-molded 37′ pilothouse cutter CORCOVADO of our design built by their father, John Guzzwell.

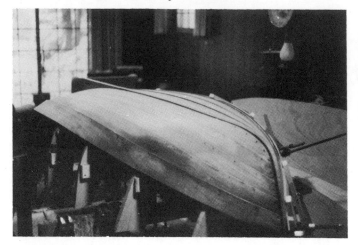

James Henning's 8′ Portland Yawlboat under construction and in use. This boat is also shown on page one. This nice looking boat fits well inside a station-wagon. Photos courtesy of the builder.

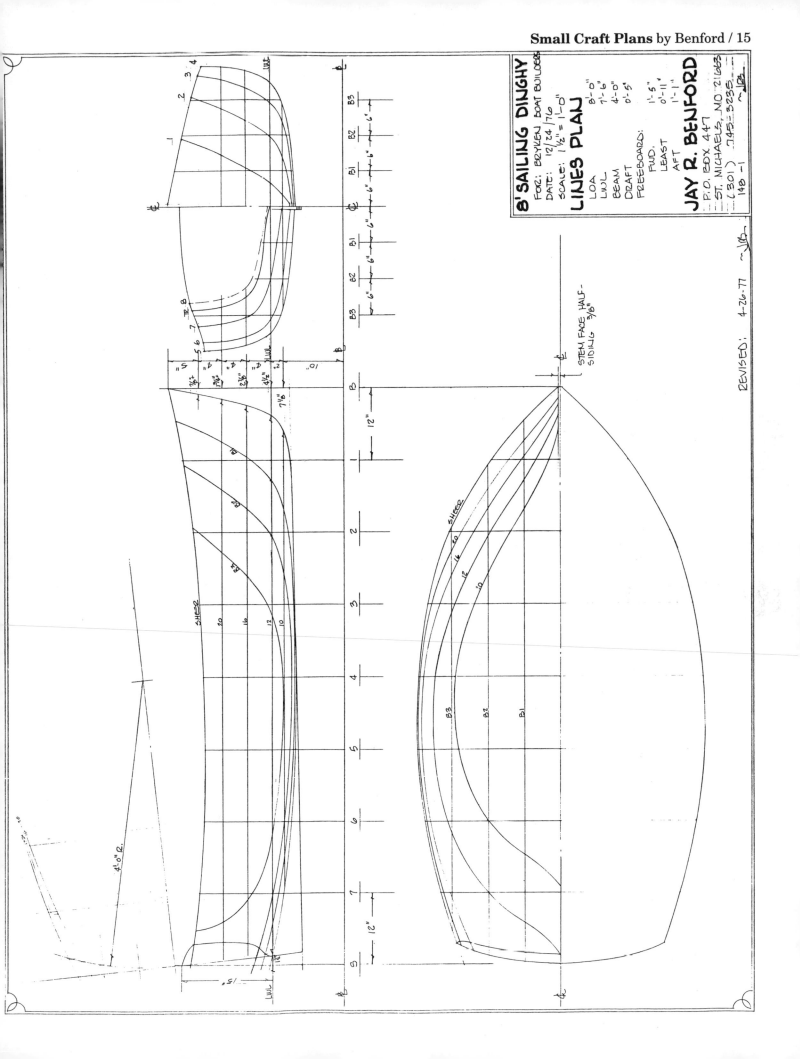

8' SAILING DINGHY

FOR: BRYKEN BOAT BUILDERS
DATE: 12/24/76
SCALE: 1½" = 1'-0"

LINES PLAN

LOA	8'-0"
LWL	7'-6"
BEAM	4'-0"
DRAFT	0'-5"
FREEBOARD:	
FWD.	1'-5"
LEAST	0'-11"
AFT	1'-1"

JAY R. BENFORD
P.O. BOX 447
ST. MICHAELS, MD 21663
(301) 745-3235
14B -1

STEM FACE HALF-
SIDING 3/8"

REVISED: 4-26-77

Offsets Table

STATION	S	7	6	5	4	3	2	1
HEIGHTS								
₵ TO FAIRBODY	1-0-3	0-10-1	0-8-6+	0-8-1	0-8-0	0-8-2	0-8-4	0-8-7
″ B1	1-1-5	0-11-0	0-9-3	0-8-4	0-8-2	0-8-4	0-9-3	1-3-3
″ B2	1-3-0	1-0-0	0-10-0	0-9-1	0-8-6	0-9-3	1-0-3	—
″ B3	1-3-3	1-3-3	0-11-5	0-10-4	0-10-2	1-0-6	2-0-1	—
″ SHEER	2-1-4	1-11-7	1-11-1	1-11-0	1-11-2+	1-11-7	2-1-0	2-2-5
HALF-BREADTHS								
₵ TO 10″ WL	—	—	1-0-0	1-4-7	1-5-3	1-2-2	0-8-1	0-1-7
″ 12″ WL	—	1-0-0	1-6-5	1-8-7	1-8-6	1-5-4	0-11-5	0-3-7
″ 16″ WL	1-1-3	1-6-2+	1-9-6	1-11-0	1-10-6	1-7-3	1-2-3	0-6-3
″ 20″ WL	1-3-3	1-7-3	1-10-1+	1-11-5	1-11-3	1-9-3	1-4-3	0-8-5
″ SHEER	1-4-0	1-7-7	1-10-4	1-11-7	1-11-5	1-10-0	1-6-3	0-11-3

NOTES:

1. LINES & OFFSETS IN FEET-INCHES-EIGHTHS TO OUTSIDE OF HULL. DEDUCT FOR SHELL THICKNESS AS DIRECTED.

2. LINES MUST BE LOFTED & FAIRED FULL SIZE — DO NOT SCALE PRINTS & OFFSETS.

3. ANY ALTERATION FROM THESE PLANS RELIEVES THE DESIGNERS FROM ANY FURTHER RESPONSIBILITY.

4. THESE PLANS ARE THE PROPERTY OF THE DESIGNERS & MAY BE USED ONLY AS AUTHORIZED BY THE DESIGNERS IN WRITING.

5. IT IS UNDERSTOOD THAT NO MORE THAN ONE BOAT WILL BE BUILT FROM THESE PLANS WITHOUT WRITTEN PERMISSION FROM THE DESIGNERS.

6. THE CORRECT METHOD OF EXPANDING & FAIRING THE TRANSOM IS SHOWN IN STEWARD'S BOATBUILDING MANUAL ON PAGES 66 & 67. EXTEND UP FROM INTERSECTIONS OF STATIONS & WL's IN SAME MANNER AS SHOWN FOR SHEER.

7. OFFSETS AT STATION 5 FOR FAIRING PURPOSES ONLY.

8' SAILING DINGHY

FOR: BRYKEU BOAT BUILT
DATE: 2-4-77
SCALE: AS NOTED

OFFSETS & NOTES

LOA	8'-0"
LWL	7'-6"
BEAM	4'-0"
DRAFT	0'-5"
FREEBOARD:	
FWD.	1'-5"
LEAST	0'-11"
AFT	1'-1"

JAY R. BENFORD
P.O. BOX 447
ST. MICHAELS, MD 21663
(301) 745-3235
148-2

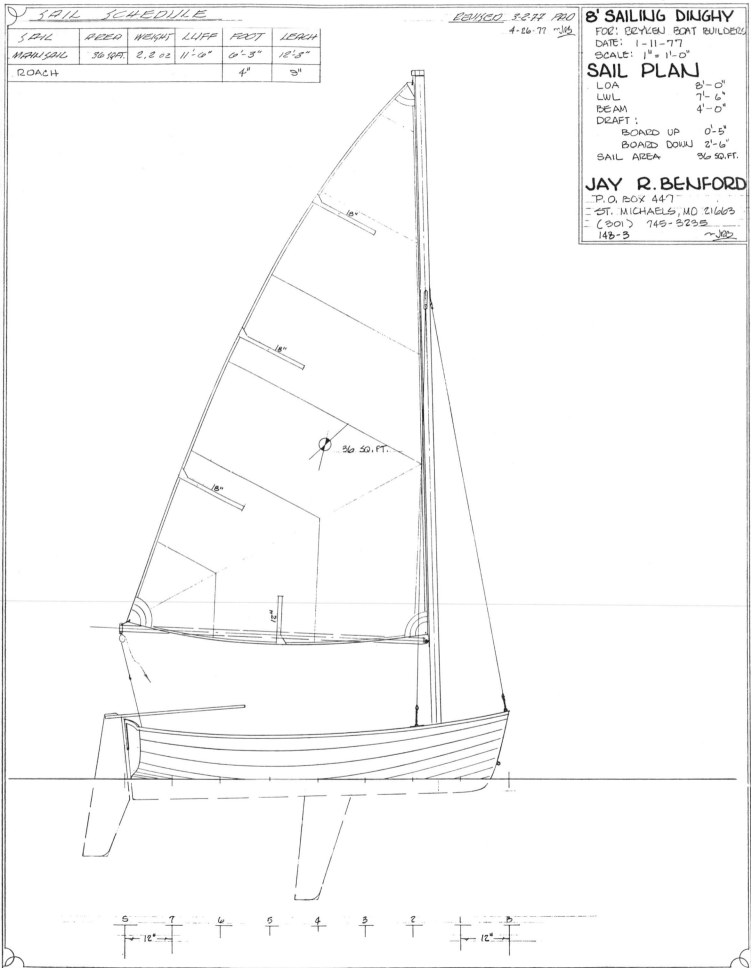

SAIL SCHEDULE

SAIL	AREA	WEIGHT	LUFF	FOOT	LEACH
MAINSAIL	36 SQ.FT.	2.2 oz	11'-6"	6'-3"	12'-8"
ROACH				4"	9"

REVISED 3-2-77 PBD
4-26-77 ~JRB

8' SAILING DINGHY
FOR: BRYKEN BOAT BUILDERS
DATE: 1-11-77
SCALE: 1" = 1'-0"

SAIL PLAN
LOA   8'-0"
LWL   7'-6"
BEAM   4'-0"
DRAFT :
    BOARD UP   0'-5"
    BOARD DOWN 2'-6"
SAIL AREA   36 SQ.FT.

JAY R. BENFORD
P.O. BOX 447
ST. MICHAELS, MD 21663
(301) 745-3235
14B-3   ~JRB

18"

18"

36 SQ.FT.

18"

12"

12"

12"

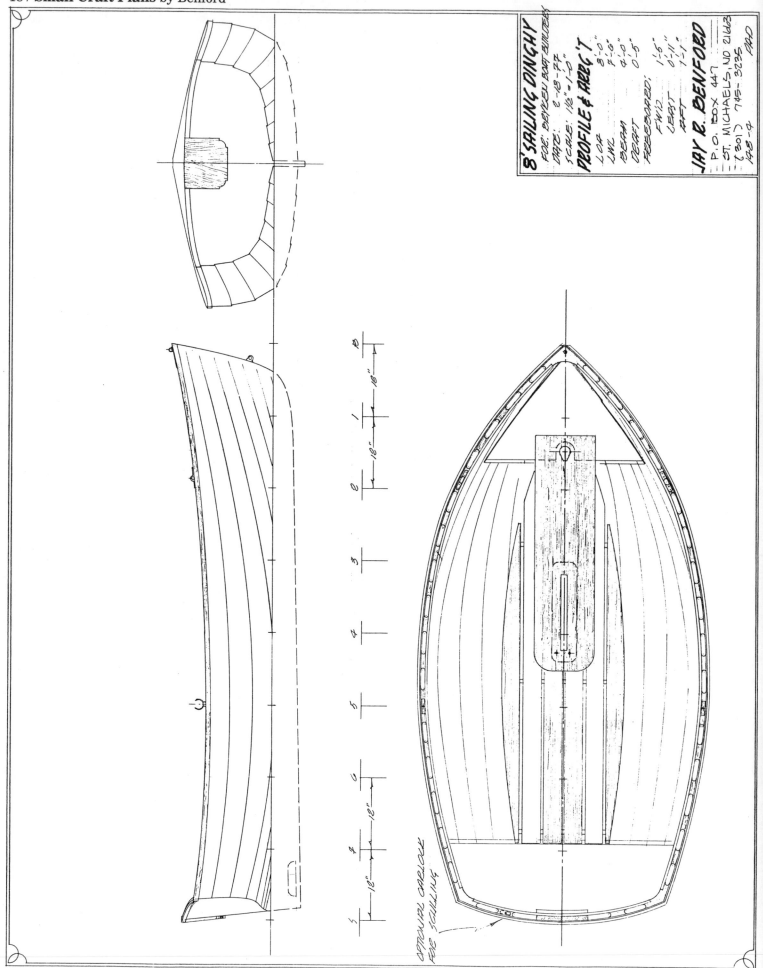

8' SAILING DINGHY

FOR: BAYDEN BOAT BUILDERS
DATE: 8-18-77
SCALE: 1½"=1'-0"

PROFILE & ARR'G'T

LOA	8'-0"
LWL	7'-6"
BEAM	4'-0"
DRAFT	0'-5"
FREEBOARD:	
FWD	1'-6"
LEAST	0'-11"
AFT	1'-1"

JAY R. BENFORD

P.O. BOX 447
ST. MICHAELS, MD 21663
(301) 745-3235

OPTIONAL CARLOW FOR SCULLING

NOTES

1. LAP OFFSETS ARE IN FEET-INCHES-EIGHTS. LAP OFF ON LOFT FLOOR FULL SIZE.
2. LAPS ARE TO PROJECT OUTSIDE OF LOFTED SECTIONS ¼" TO 5/16" AS SHOWN.
3. LAPS TO BE TAPERED OUT-BEGINNING ½" ABAFT STEM UNTIL FLUSH AT STEM.

8' SAILING DINGHY

FOR: BENFORD BOAT BUILDERS
DATE: 2-23-79
SCALE: 1½"=1'-0" # AS NOTED

PLANKING DETAILS

LOA	8'-0"
LWL	7'-6"
BEAM	4'-0"
DRAFT	5"
FREEBOARD FWD	1'-5"
LEAST	11"
AFT	1'-1"

JAY R. BENFORD
P.O. BOX 447
ST. MICHAELS, MD 21663
(301) 745-3255
748-5

LAP OFFSETS

STATION	TRANSOM	7	6	5	4	3	2	1	STEM
₵ TO LAP 1	1-10-0	1-8-5	1-7-3	1-7-1	1-7-4	1-8-3	1-10-0	2-0-3	2-3-0
₵ TO LAP 2	1-7-0	1-5-3	1-3-6	1-3-2	1-3-5	1-4-7	1-7-0	1-9-6	2-0-6
₵ TO LAP 3	1-4-2	1-2-3	1-0-0	0-11-6	1-0-4	1-1-5	1-4-0	1-7-1	1-10-2
HALF BREADTHS									
₵ TO LAP 4	1-0-4	1-1-7	1-3-7	1-5-0	1-5-2	1-4-1	1-0-2	0-7-0	—
₵ TO LAP 5	0-9-4	0-11-0	1-0-6	1-1-3	1-1-4	1-0-7	0-10-6	0-5-5	—
₵ TO LAP 6	0-6-2	0-7-0	0-8-6	0-9-6	0-9-5	0-9-1	0-8-0	0-4-3	—
₵ TO LAP 7	0-3-2	0-4-2	0-6-0	0-6-3	0-5-3	0-6-2	0-4-6	0-2-7	—

LAP DETAIL — FULL SIZE
MIN. RADIUS 1/8"
¼"
LAP 1, LAP 2, LAP 3, LAP 4, LAP 5, LAP 6, LAP 7
LOFTED SECTION

NOTES

1. LAYUP - TO BE AS FOLLOWS FROM
OUTSIDE OF SHELL TO INSIDE:
¾ oz MAT
6 oz CLOTH
¾ oz MAT
6 oz CLOTH
NOTE THAT HEAVIER REINFORCE-
MENT MAY NOT FOLLOW LAPSTRAKE
CONTOURS. DOUBLE REINFORCE-
MENT ALONG HULL & FILL
SKEG WITH URETHANE FOAM &
GLASS OVER.

2. BUOYANCY TANKS - 2 LAYERS
1½ oz MAT - BOND IN PLACE
& FILL WITH FOUR-IN-PLACE
URETHANE FOAM - COVER HOLE
WITH RUBBER PLUG.

3. OUTBOARD HANG PAD - ¾"×8½"×9"OAK
TEAK - BOND TO TRANSOM ON Ç.

4. REINFORCE DAGGERBOARD BOX
WITH ONE EXTRA LAYER OF 6 oz
CLOTH.

5. EYE BOLT - WILCOX-CRITTENDEN
FIG. 8220 1½ø×2" SHOULDER EYE BOLT -
GLASS IN WOOD BLOCK-FIT EYE BOLT -
GLASS OVER NUT.

6. TRANSFER - 3¾"×10" TEAK - CUT
SLOT FOR DAGGERBOARD

7. OUTBOARD BACKING PAD - 5/8"×8½"
×1½" TEAK - SEE SHEET 145-9

SECTION THRU
D'BOARD TRUNK
HALF SIZE

BUOYANCY TANK

8' SAILING DINGHY
FOR: BAYOU BOAT BUILDERS
DATE: 8-21-77
SCALE: 1½"=1'-0"

CONSTRUCTION

LOA   8'-0"
LWL   7'-6"
BEAM   4'-0"
DRAFT   5"
FREEBOARD FWD   1'-5"
          LEAST 11"
          AFT   1'-1"

JAY R. BENFORD
P.O. BOX 447
ST. MICHAELS, MD 21663
(301) 745-3235
145-G

MAST & OARS 1½"ø

GLASS OVER
FOAM

POUR IN PLACE
URETHANE FOAM

¾"×1" TEAK (SCREW FASTEN)

10" TRANSOM

SKEG DETAIL
HALF SIZE

MOLDED-IN MAST STEP

MOLDED IN HAND HOLD

ADD 1-4" WIDE
6 oz CLOTH TAPE
EA. SIDE D'BOARD
TRUNK

SEE SHEET 145-9
FOR GUNWALE DETAIL

DAGGERBOARD
BOX FLANGE

TRANSOM WATERLINE

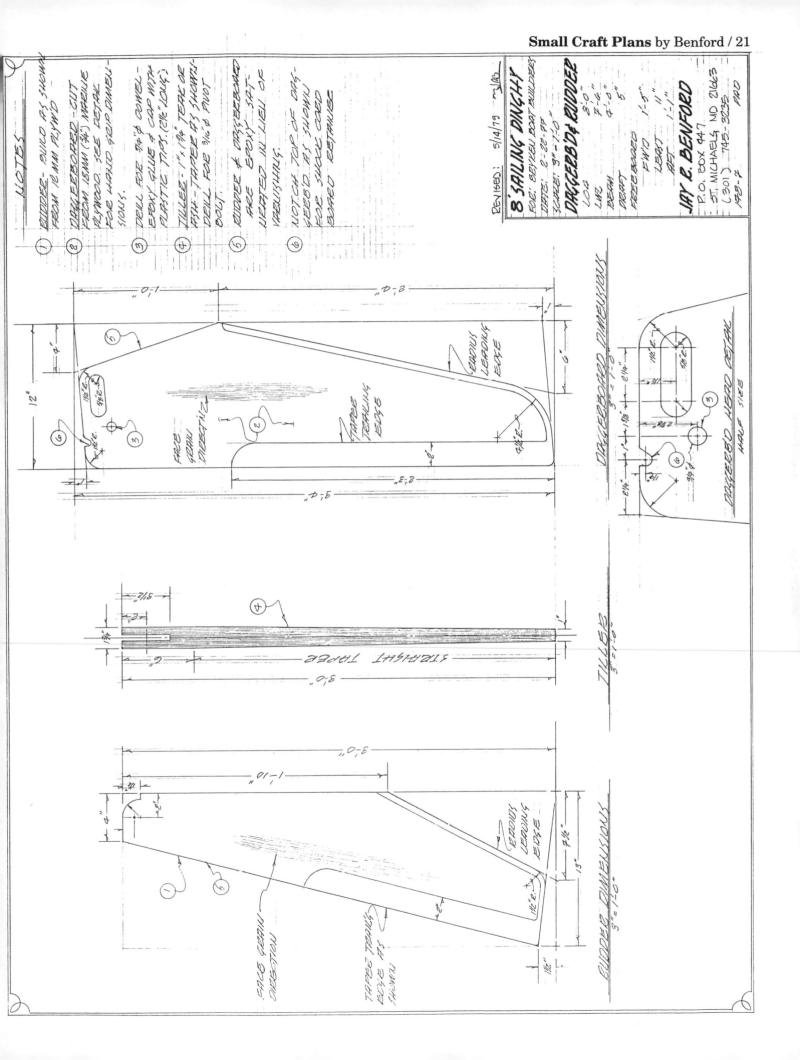

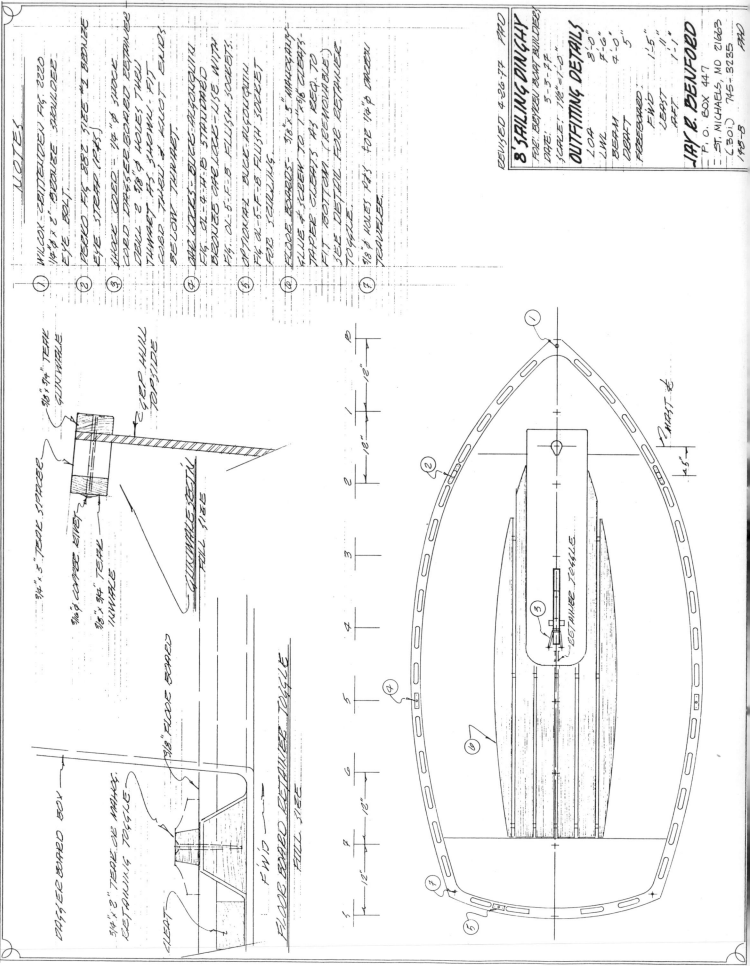

NOTES:

1. WILCOX CRITTENDEN F4, 0220 1/4"Ø 2" BRONZE SHOULDER EYE BOLT.

2. PERKO F4, 882 TEE "L" BRONZE EYE STRAP (PR.)

3. SHOCK CORD - 1/2"Ø SHOCK CORD DRESERBOARD RETAINER. DRILL 2 5/8"Ø HOLES THRU THWART FT. SHOWN - FIT CORD THRU W/ KNOTS ENDS BELOW THWART.

4. OAR LOCKS - BUCC-ALGONQUIN F4, OL-4-H-B STARBOARD BRONZE OAR LOCK - USE WITH F4, OL-5-F-B FLUSH SOCKETS.

5. OPTIONAL BUCC-ALGONQUIN F4, OL-5-F-B FLUSH SOCKET FOR SCULLING.

6. FLOOR BOARDS - 3/8" x 3" MAHOGANY - GLUE & SCREW TO 1" x 5/8" CLEATS - TAPER CLEATS AS REQ'D TO FIT BOTTOM (REMOVABLE) SEE DETAIL FOR RETAINER TOGGLE.

7. 5/8"Ø HOLES P&S FOR 1/2"Ø DINGHY TRAILER.

JAY R. BENFORD

8' SAILING DINGHY
FOR: BAYDELL BOAT BUILDERS
DATE: 5-3-77
SCALE: 1½"=1'-0"

OUTFITTING DETAILS

LOA	8'-0"
LWL	7'-6"
BEAM	4'-0"
DRAFT	5"
FREEBOARD:	
FWD	1'-5"
LEAST	11"
AFT	1'-1"

P. O. BOX 447
ST. MICHAELS, MD 21663
(301) 745-3235
145-B

NOTES

1. MAST TUBE - KENYON "A" SECTION 14'-10" LONG.
2. MAST HEAD - KENYON FIG. SM-A2N
3. MAST STEP - KENYON STANDARD MAST STEP FIG. A-111.
4. BOOM - 1½" O.D. x .065 WALL ALU. TUBE 6'-3" LONG.
5. GOOSENECK - KENYON FIG. 1-½-3-781.
6. BOOM END - KENYON FIG. SM-1-½-444.
7. MAST TANGS - KENYON FIG. SM-354-3 OR SIMILAR - 3 REQ. FASTEN TO MAST WITH RIVETS OR #10 SELF TAPPING SCREWS - LOCATE CLEVIS PIN HOLE ¢ 10'-0" ABV. MAST STEP.
8. STANDING RIGGING - 4/10" ⌀ 7 x 7 S.S. - NICO PRESS 1/10" THIMBLES EA END - WIRES 8'-2" LONG -
9. LASH STANDING RIGGING TO CHAINPLATE EYES WITH 1/8" ⌀ DACRON LINE.
10. SHROUD EYE STRAPS - PERKO FIG. 882 SIZE #1 BRONZE EYE STRAPS - FASTEN WITH 2 BOLTS ¢ 2 SCREWS.
11. HALYARD CLEAT - SCHAEFER FIG. 70-15 OR SIMILAR.
12. SHEET BLOCK - SCHAEFER FIG. 01-05 OR SIMILAR.
13. WILCOX-CRITTENDEN FIG. 341 BRASS BABY BOAT SNAP.
14. RUNNING RIGGING - ALL RUNN'G RIGGING TO BE 3/16" ⌀ DACRON BRAID.
15. OPTIONAL JOINTED MAST - SEE DETAIL - CUT MAST SLEEVE FROM .063" TYPE 6061-T6 ALU SHEET ¢ ROLL TO SHAPE - FASTEN TO TOP MAST SECTION WITH 8 RIVETS AS SHOWN.
16. TRAVELER - 1/4" ⌀ DACRON BRAID.

8' SAILING DINGHY
FOR: BRYKEN BOAT BUILDERS
DATE: 3-2-77
SCALE: 1"=1'-0"

SPARS & RIGGING

LOA	8'-0"
LWL	7'-6"
BEAM	4'-0"
DRAFT	
BOARD UP	5"
BOARD D'N	2'-6"
SAIL AREA	36 SQ.FT.

JAY R. BENFORD
P.O. BOX 447
ST. MICHAELS, MD 21663
(301) 745-3235
M8-9   VRD

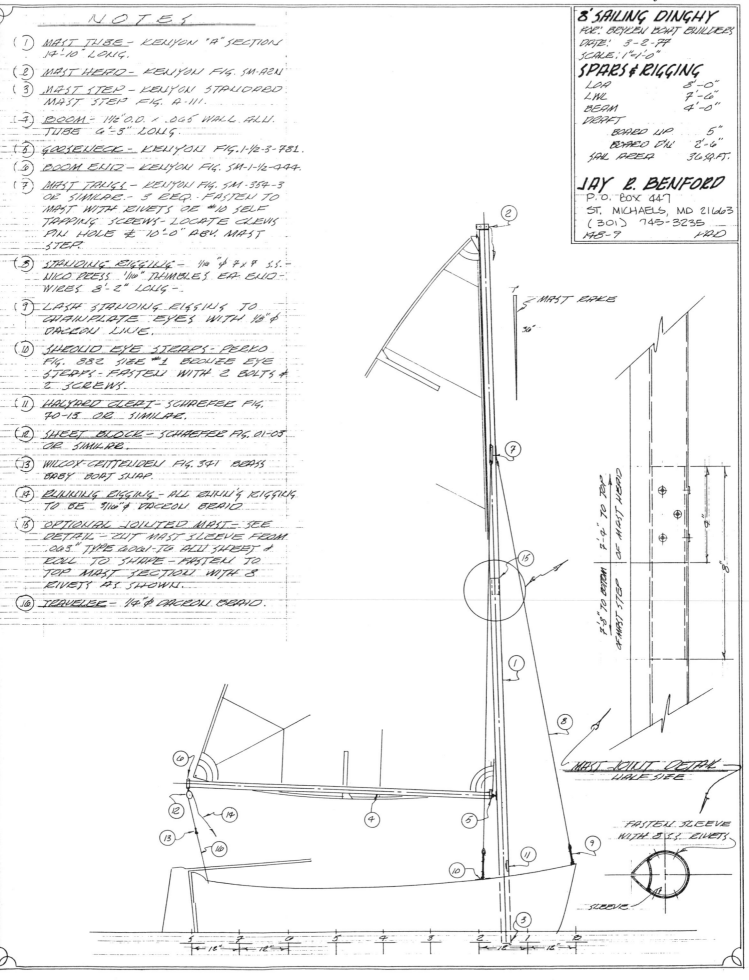

MAST RAKE

36"

F'-8" TO BOTTOM   F'-9" TO TOP
OF MAST STEP   OF MAST HEAD

MAST JOINT DETAIL
HALF SIZE

FASTEN SLEEVE
WITH 8 S.S. RIVETS

SLEEVE

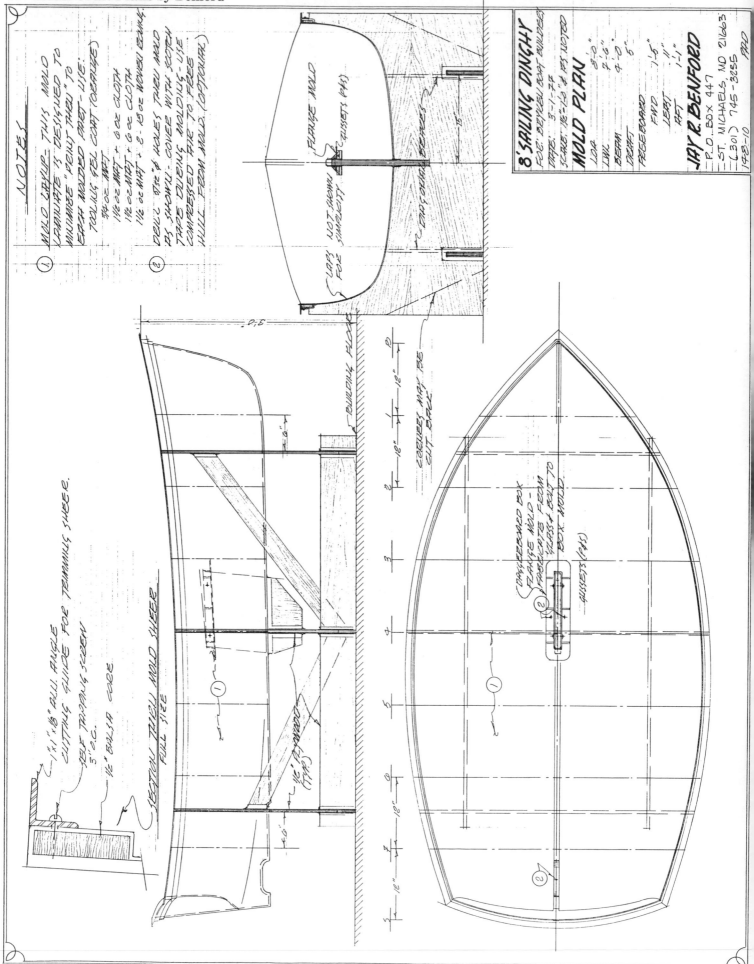

NOTES

1. MOLD LAYUP: THIS MOLD LAMINATE IS DESIGNED TO MINIMIZE "PRINT THRU" TO EACH MOLDED PART. USE:
   TOOLING GEL COAT (ORANGE)
   3/4 oz MAT
   1½ oz MAT + 6 oz CLOTH
   1½ oz MAT + 6 oz CLOTH
   1½ oz MAT + 8 · 15 oz WOVEN ROVING.

2. DRILL 3/16" Ø HOLES THRU MOLD AS SHOWN - COVER WITH SCOTCH TAPE DURING MOLDING - USE COMPRESSED AIR TO FREE HULL FROM MOLD. (OPTIONAL)

8' SAILING DINGHY

FOR: BENGAL BOAT BUILDERS
DATE: 3·1·77
SCALE: 1½"=1' SEE NOTES

MOLD PLAN

COLOR: LIGHT BLUE

LOA   8'·0"
LWL   7'·6"
BEAM   4'·0"
DRAFT   5"
FREEBOARD
  FWD   1'·5"
  LEAST   11"
  AFT   1'·1"

JAY R. BENFORD

P.O. BOX 447
ST. MICHAELS, MD 21663
(301) 745·3255
1978·10
PRO

FLANGE MOLD

GUSSETS (TYP)

LAPS NOT SHOWN FOR SIMPLICITY

CAP OUTBOARD EDGES

BUILDING FLOOR

0'·0"

6"

0"

12"

12"

1

12"

2

2

3

CORNERS MAY BE CUT OFF.

4

5

6

12"

7

8

12"

DAGGERBOARD BOX - FLANGE MOLD - FABRICATE FROM GLASS & BOLT TO BOX MOLD.

GUSSETS (TYP)

1

2

1 × 1 × 1/8" ALU. ANGLE CUTTING GUIDE FOR TRIMMING SHEER.

SELF TAPPING SCREW 5" O.C.

½" BALSA CORE

SECTION THRU MOLD SHEER
FULL SIZE

½" PLYWOOD (TYP)

1

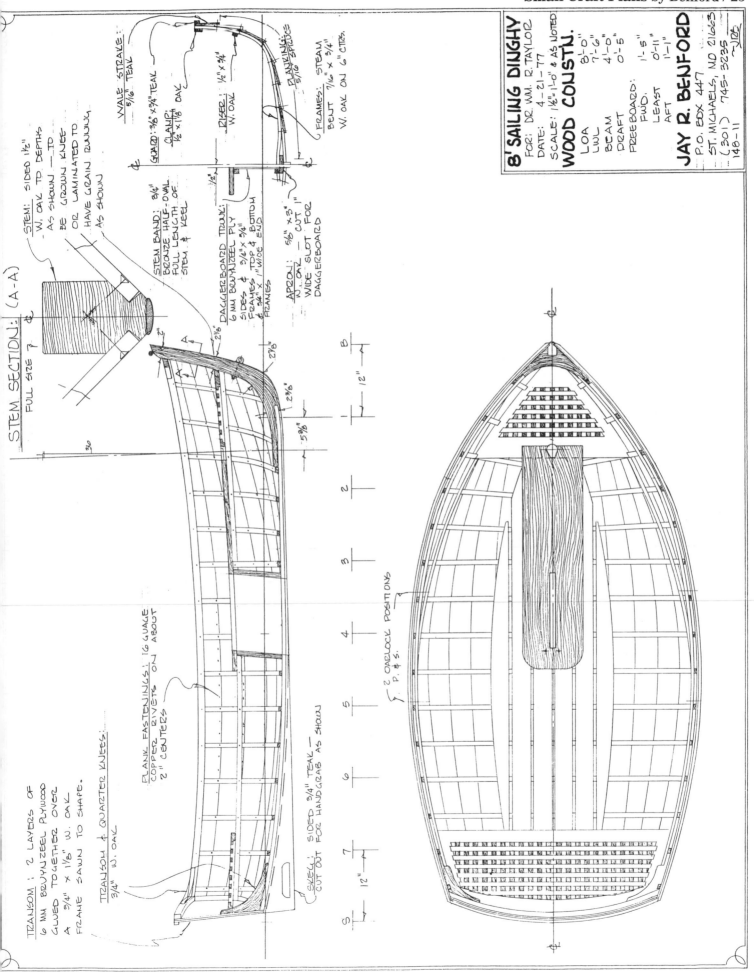

TRANSOM: 2 LAYERS OF
6 MM BRUYNZEEL PLYWOOD
GLUED TOGETHER OVER
A 3/4" x 1 1/8" W. OAK
FRAME SAWN TO SHAPE.

TRANSOM & QUARTER KNEES:
3/4" W. OAK

PLANK FASTENINGS: 16 GUAGE
COPPER RIVETS ON ABOUT
2" CENTERS

SKEG: SIDED 3/4" TEAL —
CUT OUT FOR HANDGRAB AS SHOWN

STEM SECTION: (A-A)
FULL SIZE ?

STEM: SIDED 1 1/2"
— W. OAK TO DEPTHS
AS SHOWN — TO
BE GROWN KNEE
OR LAMINATED TO
HAVE GRAIN RUNNING
AS SHOWN

WALE STRAKE:
5/16 TEAL

GUARD: 3/8" x 3/4" TEAL

CLAMP:
1/2 x 1 1/8" OAK

RISER: 1/2" x 3/4"
W. OAK

PLANKING:
5/16 SPRUCE

FRAMES: STEAM
BENT 7/16" x 3/4"
W. OAK ON 6" CTRS.

STEM BAND: 3/4"
BRONZE HALF-OVAL
FULL LENGTH OF
STEM & KEEL

DAGGERBOARD TRUNK:
6 MM BRUYNZEEL PLY
SIDES & 3/4" x 3/4"
FRAMES, TOP & BOTTOM
& 3/4" x 1" WIDE END
FRAMES

APRON: 5/8" x 3"
W. OAK - CUT 1"
WIDE - SLOT FOR
DAGGERBOARD

2 OARLOCK POSITIONS
P. & S.

8' SAILING DINGHY
FOR: DR. WM. R. TAYLOR
DATE: 4-21-77
SCALE: 1 1/2"=1'-0" & AS NOTED
WOOD CONSTN.

LOA	8'-0"
LWL	7'-6"
BEAM	4'-0"
DRAFT	0-5"
FREEBOARD:	
FWD.	1'-5"
LEAST	0'-11"
AFT	1'-1"

JAY R. BENFORD
P.O. BOX 447
ST. MICHAELS, MD 21663
(301) 745-3235
146-11

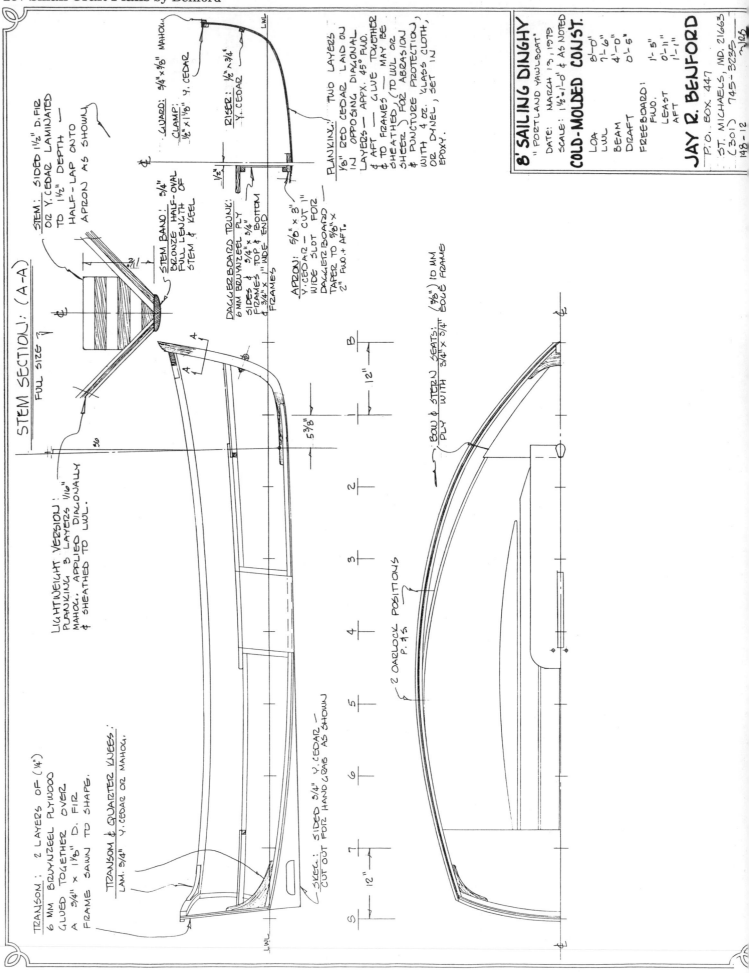

STEM SECTION: (A-A)
FULL SIZE

STEM: SIDED 1½" D. FIR
OR Y. CEDAR LAMINATED
TO 1½" DEPTH —
HALF-LAP ONTO
APRON AS SHOWN

GUARD: 5/4" x 7/8" MAHOG.

CLAMP:
½" x 1⅛" Y. CEDAR

RISER: ½" x ¾"
Y. CEDAR

STEM BAND: ¼"
BRONZE HALF-OVAL
FULL LENGTH OF
STEM & KEEL

DAGGER BOARD TRUNK:
6 MM BRONZEEL PLY
SIDES & ¾" x 5/4"
FRAMES TOP & BOTTOM
& ¾" x 1" WIDE END
FRAMES

APRON: 5/8 x 3"
Y. CEDAR - CUT 1"
WIDE SLOT FOR
DAGGER BOARD
TAPER TO 5/8" x
2" FWD. & AFT.

PLANKING: TWO LAYERS
1/8" RED CEDAR LAID ON
IN OPPOSING DIAGONAL
LAYERS — APPX. 45° FWD.
& AFT — GLUE TOGETHER
& TO FRAMES MAY BE
SHEATHED (TO WL OR
SHEER) FOR ABRASION
& PUNCTURE PROTECTION,
WITH 4 OZ. 'GLASS CLOTH,
OR DYNEL, SET IN
EPOXY.

TRANSOM: 2 LAYERS OF (¼")
6 MM BRONZEEL PLYWOOD
GLUED TOGETHER OVER
A 5/4" x 1⅛" D. FIR
FRAME SAWN TO SHAPE.

TRANSOM & QUARTER KNEES:
LAM. 5/4" Y. CEDAR OR MAHOG.

LIGHTWEIGHT VERSION:
PLANKING 3 LAYERS 1/16"
MAHOG. APPLIED DIAGONALLY
& SHEATHED TO WL.

SKEG: SIDED 5/4" Y. CEDAR —
CUT OUT FOR HANDGRAB AS SHOWN

BOW & STERN SEATS: (7/8") TO MM
PLY WITH ¾" x 5/4"
EDGE FRAME

2 OARLOCK POSITIONS
P. 15.

12"   5/8"   12"

LWL

8' SAILING DINGHY
"PORTLAND YAWLBOAT"

DATE: MARCH 13, 1979

SCALE: 1½"=1'-0" & AS NOTED

COLD-MOLDED CONST.

LOA	8'-0"
LWL	7'-6"
BEAM	4'-0"
DRAFT	0'-6"

FREEBOARD:
FWD.	1'-5"
LEAST	0'-11"
AFT	1'-1"

JAY R. BENFORD

P.O. BOX 447
ST. MICHAELS, MD. 21663
(301) 745-3235
148-12

Mike Kiefer's 8-footer (below) shows fine detailing. He builds these and other dinghies at Great Lakes Boatbuilding Co. in South Haven, Michigan. Photo courtesy of the builder.

Chapter 5
8 1/2′ Dinghy

This design was originally planned to have a miniature steam engine in her. Our client was in the business of building large steam engines, including some at Disney facilities and some large locomotive replicas. However, he ultimately decided to just do her as a rowing or outboard powered boat.

The design evolved from the 8′ Portland Yawlboat. She was made a couple inches deeper to carry more of a load and the stem was moved about six inches forward. The net effect of this was to make her a better carrier, and the finer entry will make her row and sail even better.

The sailplan, rudder and daggerboard are all lifted directly from the 8′ Portland Yawlboat, and the construction detailing from the 8-footer can be used for this boat as well.

Carl Brownstein of Rights O'Man Boat Works built her at Shelton, Washington, and the photos show what a nice job he did. The centerline combination seat and locker is for the small engine and/or other equipment.

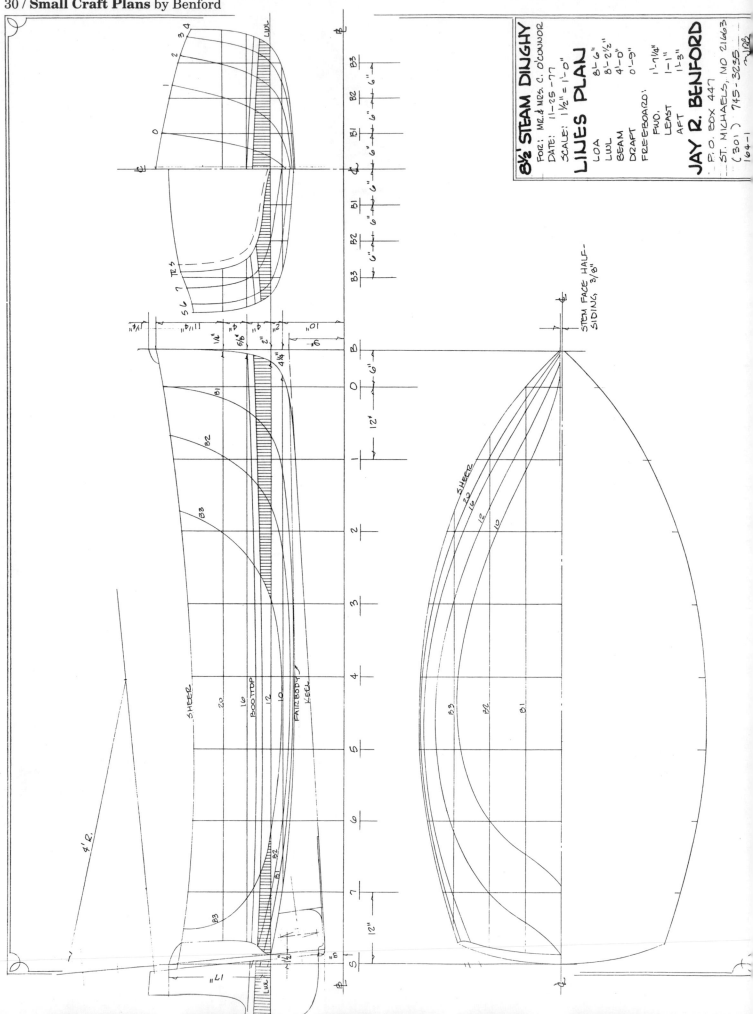

8½' STEAM DINGHY

FOR: MR. & MRS. C. O'CONNOR

DATE: 11-25-77

SCALE: 1½" = 1'-0"

LINES PLAN

LOA	8'-6"
LWL	8'-2½"
BEAM	4'-0"
DRAFT	0'-9"
FREEBOARD:	
FWD.	1'-7¼"
LEAST	1'-1"
AFT	1'-3"

JAY R. BENFORD

P.O. BOX 447

ST. MICHAELS, MD 21663

(301) 745-3235

164-1

NOTES:

1. LINES & OFFSETS IN FEET – INCHES – EIGHTHS – TO OUTSIDE OF HULL – DEDUCT FOR SHELL THICKNESS AS DIRECTED.

2. LINES MUST BE LOFTED & FAIRED FULL SIZE — DO NOT SCALE PRINTS & OFFSETS.

3. ANY ALTERATION FROM THESE PLANS RELIEVES THE DESIGNERS FROM ANY FURTHER RESPONSIBILITY.

4. THESE PLANS ARE THE PROPERTY OF THE DESIGNERS & MAY BE USED ONLY AS AUTHORIZED BY THE DESIGNERS IN WRITING.

5. IT IS UNDERSTOOD THAT NO MORE THAN ONE BOAT WILL BE BUILT FROM THESE PLANS WITHOUT WRITTEN PERMISSION FROM THE DESIGNERS.

6. THE CORRECT METHOD OF EXPANDING & FAIRING THE TRANSOM IS SHOWN IN STEWARD'S BOATBUILDING MANUAL ON PAGES 66 & 67. EXTEND UP FROM INTERSECTIONS OF STATIONS & WL'S IN SAME MANNER AS SHOWN FOR SHEER.

7. OFFSETS AT STATION S FOR FAIRING PURPOSES ONLY.

8. BOOTTOP OFFSETS TO TOP EDGE OF STRIPE — STRIPE IS 1" HIGH IN PROFILE FULL LENGTH.

8½' STEAM DINGHY

FOR: MR. & MRS. C. O'CONNOR
DATE: 11-25-77
SCALE: AS NOTED

OFFSETS & NOTES

LOA	8'-6"
LWL	8'-2½"
BEAM	4'-0"
DRAFT	0'-5"
FREEBOARD:	
FWD.	
LEAST	
AFT	

JAY R. BENFORD
P.O. BOX 447
ST. MICHAELS, MD. 21663
(301) 745-3235
164-2

STATION	S	7	6	5	4	3	2	1	0
HEIGHTS									
℄ TO FAIRBODY	1-0-3	0-10-1	0-8-6+	0-8-1	0-8-0	0-8-1-	0-8-3-	0-8-5	0-9-3
" B1	1-1-5	0-11-0	0-9-3	0-8-4	0-8-2	0-8-3-	0-9-0	0-10-3	2-4-6
" B2	1-3-0	1-0-0	0-10-0	0-9-1	0-8-6	0-9-1	0-10-5	1-7-1	—
" B3	—	1-3-3	0-11-5	0-10-4	0-10-2	0-11-6+	1-8-4	—	—
" SHEER	2-3-4	2-1-7	2-1-1	2-1-0	2-1-2+	2-1-7+	2-2-7+	2-4-3	2-6-1
" BOOTTOP	1-3-3+	1-2-7	1-2-4+	1-2-3+	1-2-4	1-2-5	1-2-7	1-3-2	1-3-5+
HALF-BREADTHS									
℄ TO 10"WL	—	—	1-0-0	1-4-7	1-5-3	1-2-7	0-10-6	0-5-1	0-0-5+
" 12"WL	—	1-0-0	1-6-5	1-8-7	1-8-6	1-6-1+	1-1-7	0-8-1-	0-2-0
" 16"WL	1-1-3	1-6-2+	1-9-5	1-11-0	1-10-6	1-8-4+	1-4-3+	0-10-5+	0-5-5
" 20"WL	1-3-3	1-7-3	1-10-1+	1-11-5	1-11-3	1-9-4	1-5-7	1-0-2	0-4-5
" SHEER	1-4-0	1-7-7	1-10-4	1-11-7	1-11-5	1-10-3	1-1-2	1-2-1	0-6-1

NOTES

1. LAP OFFSETS ARE IN FEET, INCHES, AND EIGHTHS. LAY OFF ON LOFT FLOOR FULL SIZE.

2. LAPS ARE TO PROJECT OUTSIDE OF LOFTED SECTIONS ¼" TO 5⁄16" AS SHOWN.

3. LAPS TO BE TAPERED OUT BEGINNING 6" ABAFT STEM, UNTIL FLUSH AT STEM.

LAP OFFSETS

STATION	TRANSOM	7	6	5	4	3	2	1	0
HEIGHTS									
℔ TO LAP 1	2-0-4	1-11-1	1-10-1	1-9-7	1-10-1	1-10-7	2-0-1+	2-1-6+	2-5-6
℔ TO LAP 2	1-10-0	1-8-5	1-7-3+	1-7-1	1-7-3	1-8-2	1-9-5	1-11-4	2-1-5
℔ TO LAP 3	1-7-0	1-5-2	1-3-5	1-3-1	1-3-3+	1-4-5	1-6-3	1-8-4	1-11-1
HALF BREADTHS									
℄ TO LAP 4	1-3-1	1-4-7	1-7-1	1-8-1	1-8-6-	1-7-1	1-5-7	1-1-3	0-4-6
℄ TO LAP 5	1-0-5	1-2-0+	1-3-6	1-5-0	1-5-2	1-4-3+	1-2-1	0-10-2	0-4-2
℄ TO LAP 6	0-9-4+	0-11-0	1-0-4+	1-1-3	1-1-3+	1-0-6+	0-11-3	0-8-4	0-5-4
℄ TO LAP 7	0-6-4	0-7-6	0-8-6	0-9-3	0-9-4+	0-9-3	0-8-3+	0-6-4+	0-2-7
℄ TO LAP 8	0-3-1+	0-4-2	0-5-1	0-5-4	0-5-4	0-5-3	0-4-7	0-4-1	0-2-0

BASE LINE

MIN. RADIUS ⅛"

LAP DETAIL — LAP 8 FULL SIZE

LOFTED SECTION

LAP 1 — LAP 2 — LAP 3 — LAP 4 — LAP 5 — LAP 6 — LAP 7 — LAP 8

PLANKING DETAILS

8½' SAILING DINGHY
FOR: MR. & MRS. C. O'CONNOR
DATE: 2-18-84
SCALE: 1½" = 1'-0" & AS NOTED

LOA	8'-6"
LWL	8'-2½"
BEAM	4'-0"
DRAFT	0'-9"

FREEBOARD:
FWD. 1'-7¼"
LEAST 1'-1"
AFT 1'-3"

JAY R. BENFORD
P.O. BOX 447
ST. MICHAELS, MD. 21663
(301) 745-3235

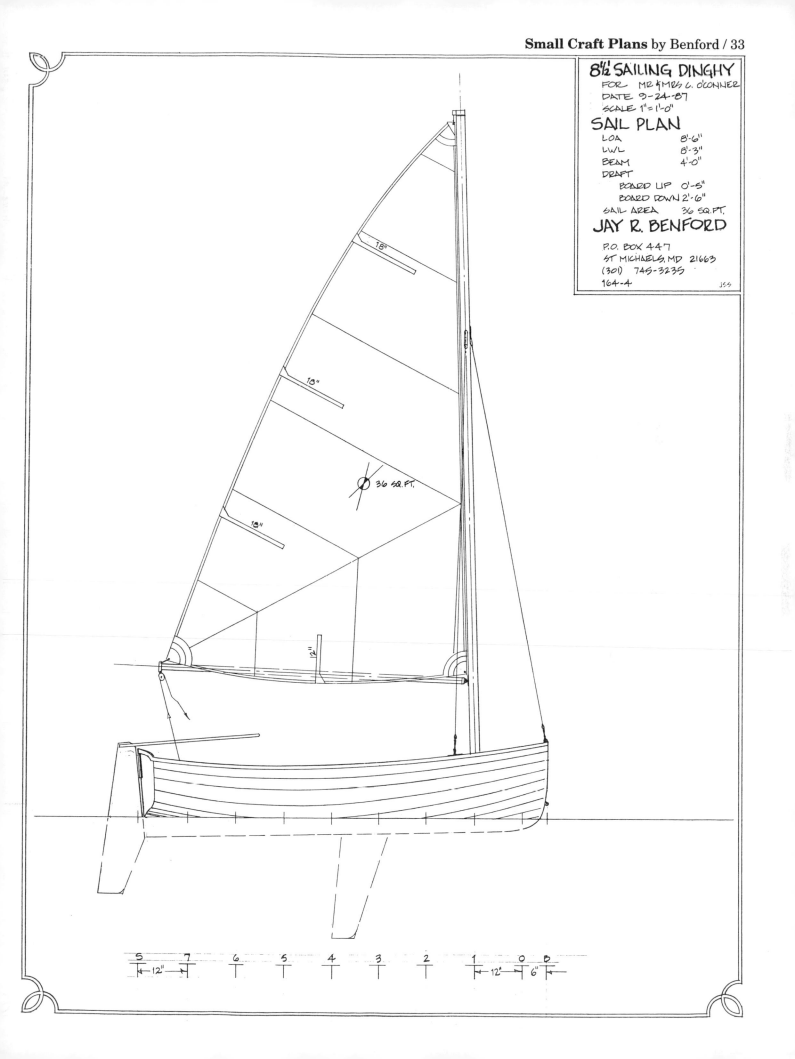

8½' SAILING DINGHY
FOR MR & MRS L. O'CONNER
DATE 9-24-87
SCALE 1"=1'-0"

SAIL PLAN
LOA   8'-6"
LWL   8'-3"
BEAM   4'-0"
DRAFT
    BOARD UP 0'-5"
    BOARD DOWN 2'-6"
SAIL AREA   36 SQ.FT.

JAY R. BENFORD
P.O. BOX 447
ST MICHAELS, MD 21663
(301) 745-3235
164-4   JSS

18"

18"

36 SQ.FT.

18"

12"

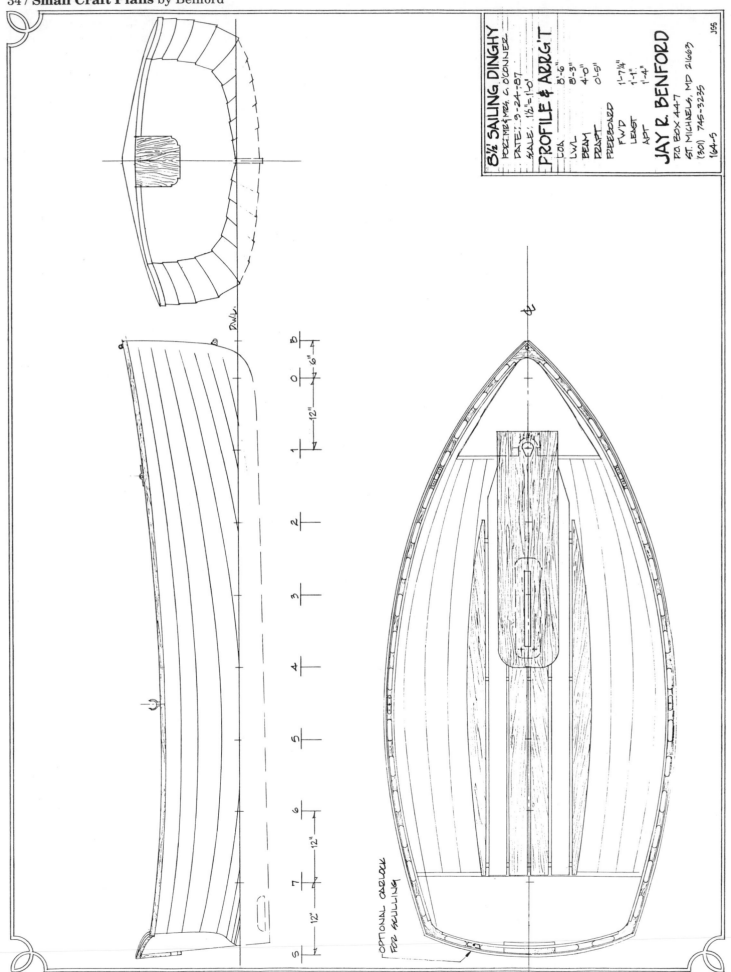

8½' SAILING DINGHY

FOR: MEG & MEG., G. O'CONNER

DATE: 9-24-87

SCALE: 1½"=1'-0"

PROFILE & ARRG'T

LOA	8'-6"
LWL	8'-3"
BEAM	4'-0"
DRAFT	0'-5"
FREEBOARD	
FW'D	1'-7¼"
LEAST	1'-1"
AFT	1'-4"

JAY R. BENFORD

P.O. BOX 447

ST. MICHAELS, MD 21663

(301) 745-3235

164-5

J55

OPTIONAL OARLOCK
FOR SCULLING

Chapter 6
9′ Pacific Peapod

Seven years after we'd done the 11′ Oregon Peapod (see chapter 8), another builder asked us for a smaller version. Many of our design commissions come about this way, with someone seeing a boat they like, and then asking for a boat like it either smaller or larger. We also get commissions for modified versions, and some of the plans in this book show different construction plans. These are the result of people wanting to build the boats in differing methods. If we think the request is reasonable, we are usually happy to undertake the commission to convert the design.

The original plan was to produce this boat in fiberglass. As occassionally happens, their plans got delayed and they haven't built the boat yet.

However, I've liked the design well enough to have speculated the time to finish off the construction detailing.

The construction called for is cold-molding, which produces a light and strong boat. This is probably the best choice for a one-off, if the builder is not experienced in other techniques. She could also be done in lapstrake or Airex-cored fiberglass. The scantlings for the other small boats in this book would be suitable for these alternatives.

The daggerboard slot comes down alongside the centerline skeg, so this will not have to be weakened with a cut through it. A tee shaped slot cap should be made for use when the boat is being towed or under outboard power. This will keep water from splashing through and eventually flooding the boat.

If she is to be towed, the towing eye should be fitted about three inches above the datum waterline (noted as DWL on the drawings). This will help hold her head up making towing easier. Be sure to through bolt the towing eye to a backing plate for maximum strength.

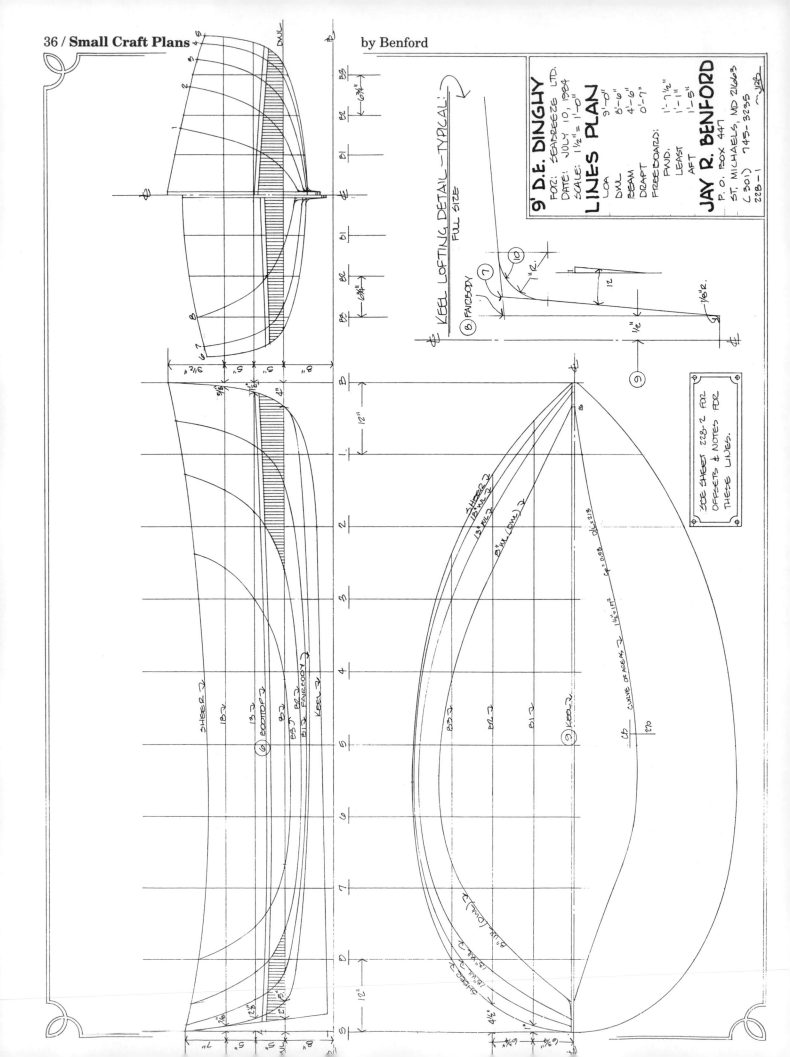

STATION	S	B	7	6	5	4	3	2	1	B
				H E I G H T S						
℄ TO KEEL	(0-1-0)	0-1-3	0-1-0	1-2-0	2-4-0	2-2-0	0-3-2	0-3-5	0-4-0	2-3-2
℄ TO FAIRBODY	2-1-0	0-5-7	0-4-7	0-4-2	0-3-7	0-3-7	0-4-1	0-4-5	0-5-4	2-3-4
℄ TO B1	(2-4-4)	0-7-3	0-5-4	0-4-5	0-4-4	0-4-4	0-5-1	0-6-3	0-11-0	—
℄ TO B2	—	0-10-5	0-6-3	0-5-3	0-5-3	0-5-0	0-7-0	0-11-1	0-11-1	—
℄ TO B3	—	1-10-5	0-9-1	0-7-1	0-7-2	0-8-2	1-1-0	—	—	—
DWL TO BOOTTOP	(0-4-0)	0-3-3	0-3-1	0-3-0	1-5-0	2-3-0	0-3-4	0-3-7	0-4-3	(0-5-0)
DWL TO SHEER	1-5-0	1-2-5	1-1-3	1-1-0	1-1-1	1-1-5	1-2-4	1-3-5	1-5-2	1-7-4
				H A L F - B R E A D T H S						
℄ TO 8" WL (DWL)	—	0-8-5	1-6-2	1-10-1	1-10-1	1-7-7	1-3-0	0-10-1	0-4-3	—
℄ TO 13" WL	—	1-3-5	1-11-1	2-1-5	2-1-5	1-11-7	1-8-2	1-2-7	0-7-6	—
℄ TO 18" WL	—	1-6-5	2-0-3	2-2-5	2-2-4	2-1-1	1-10-1	1-5-1	0-9-5	—
℄ TO SHEER	0-0-4	1-8-2	2-1-1	2-2-7	2-2-6	2-1-4	1-10-7	1-6-3	0-11-3	0-0-4

NOTES:

1. LINES & OFFSETS IN FEET-INCHES-EIGHTHS. OFFSETS TO OUTSIDE OF HULL. DEDUCT FOR SHELL THICKNESS AS REQUIRED.
2. LINES MUST BE LOFTED & FAIRED FULL SIZE — DO NOT SCALE OFFSETS & PRINTS.
3. ANY ALTERATION FROM THESE PLANS RELIEVES THE DESIGNER FROM ANY FURTHER RESPONSIBILITY.
4. THESE PLANS ARE THE PROPERTY OF THE DESIGNER & MAY BE USED ONLY AS AUTHORIZED BY THE DESIGNER IN WRITING.
5. IT IS UNDERSTOOD THAT NO BOATS WILL BE BUILT FROM THESE PLANS WITHOUT PAYMENT TO THE DESIGNER OF HIS ROYALTY.
6. BOOTTOP OFFSETS TO TOP EDGE OF BOOT STRIPE. STRIPE IS 3/4" HIGH IN PROFILE.
7. KEEL WIDTH AT HULL TO BE DEVELOPED ON LOFT FLOOR PER DETAIL ON SHEET 228-1. STERNPOST DONE SAME WAY HORIZONTALLY.
8. FAIRBODY IS ½" OFF ℄ AS SHOWN.
9. STEM, KEEL, & STERNPOST TO ALL HAVE ½" HALF-BREADTH ON FACE.
10. 1" RADIUS AT JOINING OF HULL TO KEEL & STERNPOST.
11. OFFSETS IN BRACKETS (0-0-0) FOR FAIRING PURPOSES ONLY.

9' D.E. DINGHY
FOR: SEABREEZE LTD.
DATE: JULY 10, 1984
SCALE: AS NOTED

OFFSETS & NOTES

LOA — 9'-0"
DWL — 8'-0"
BEAM — 4'-0"
DRAFT — 0'-7"
FREEBOARD:
 FWD. — 1'-7½"
 LEAST — 1'-1"
 AFT — 1'-5"

JAY R. BENFORD
P.O. BOX 447
ST. MICHAELS, MD 21663
(301) 745-3235
228-2

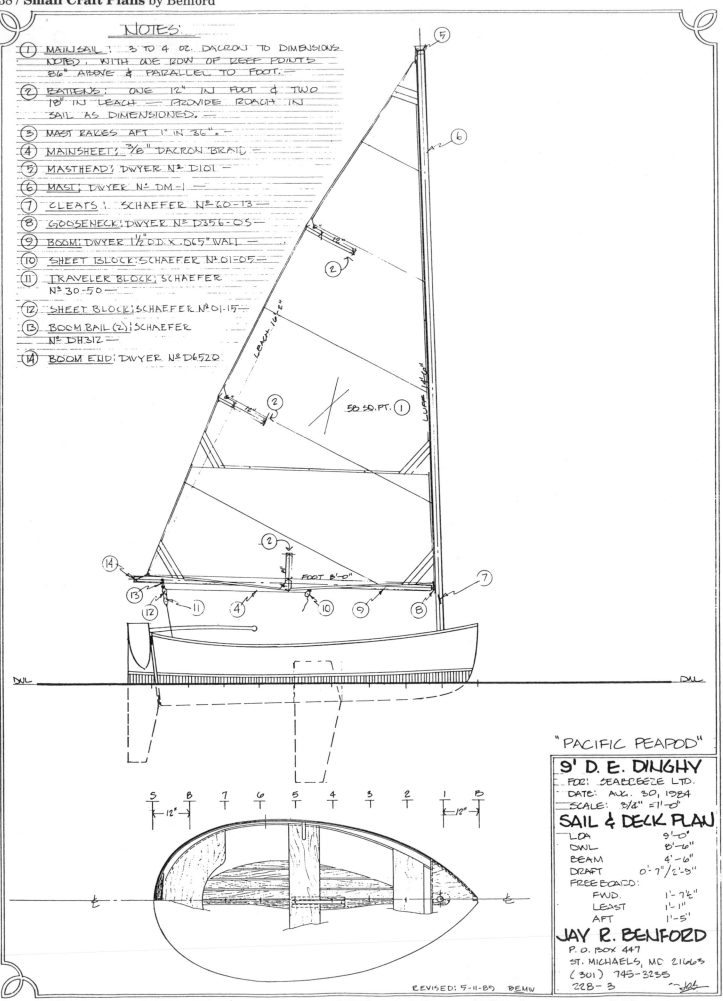

NOTES:

1. MAINSAIL: 3 TO 4 OZ. DACRON TO DIMENSIONS NOTED, WITH ONE ROW OF REEF POINTS 36" ABOVE & PARALLEL TO FOOT.

2. BATTENS: ONE 12" IN FOOT & TWO 18" IN LEACH — PROVIDE ROACH IN SAIL AS DIMENSIONED.

3. MAST RAKES AFT 1" IN 36".

4. MAINSHEET: 3/8" DACRON BRAID

5. MASTHEAD: DWYER No. D101

6. MAST: DWYER No. DM-1

7. CLEATS: SCHAEFER No. 60-13

8. GOOSENECK: DWYER No. D356-05

9. BOOM: DWYER 1½" O.D. X .065" WALL

10. SHEET BLOCK: SCHAEFER No. 01-05

11. TRAVELER BLOCK: SCHAEFER No. 30-50

12. SHEET BLOCK: SCHAEFER No. 01-15

13. BOOM BAIL (2): SCHAEFER No. DH312

14. BOOM END: DWYER No. D6520

58 SQ. FT.

FOOT 8'-0"

"PACIFIC PEAPOD"

9' D. E. DINGHY
FOR: SEABREEZE LTD.
DATE: AUG. 30, 1984
SCALE: 3/4" = 1'-0"

SAIL & DECK PLAN

LOA	9'-0"
DWL	8'-6"
BEAM	4'-6"
DRAFT	0'-7"/2'-5"
FREEBOARD:	
FWD.	1'-7½"
LEAST	1'-1"
AFT	1'-5"

JAY R. BENFORD
P. O. BOX 447
ST. MICHAELS, MD 21663
(301) 745-3235
228-3

REVISED: 5-11-89 BEMW

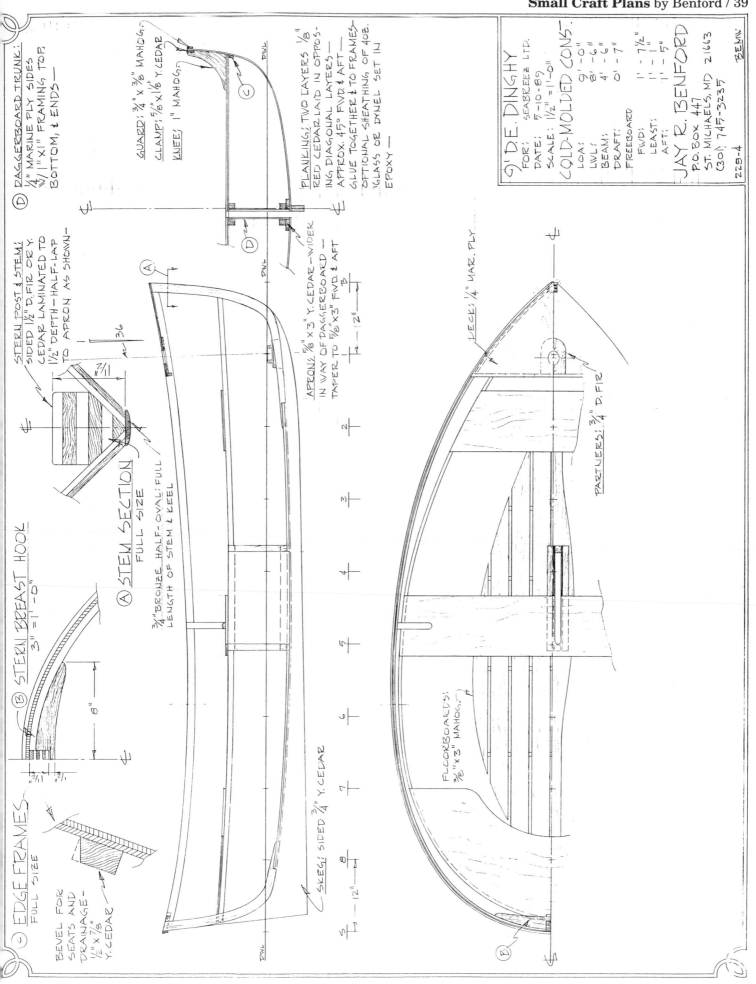

(D) DAGGERBOARD TRUNK:
1/4" MARINE PLY SIDES
W/ 1"X1" FRAMING TOP,
BOTTOM, & ENDS —

GUARD: 3/4" X 3/8" MAHOG.
CLAMP: 5/8"X1 1/8" Y. CEDAR
KNEE: 1" MAHOG.

PLANKING: TWO LAYERS 1/8"
RED CEDAR LAID IN OPPOS-
ING DIAGONAL LAYERS —
APPROX. 45° FWD & AFT —
GLUE TOGETHER & TO FRAMES —
OPTIONAL SHEATHING OF 4 OZ.
GLASS OR DYNEL SET IN
EPOXY —

STERN POST & STEM:
SIDED 1 1/2" D. FIR OR Y.
CEDAR LAMINATED TO
1 1/2" DEPTH — HALF-LAP
TO APRON AS SHOWN —

APRON: 7/8 X 3" Y. CEDAR — WIDER
IN WAY OF DAGGERBOARD —
TAPER TO 7/8"X3" FWD & AFT

(A) STEM SECTION
FULL SIZE

3/4" BRONZE HALF-OVAL FULL
LENGTH OF STEM & KEEL

(B) STERN BREAST HOOK
3" = 1'-0"

SKEG: SIDED 3/4" Y. CEDAR

(C) EDGE FRAMES
FULL SIZE

BEVEL FOR
SEATS AND
DRAINAGE —
1/2" X 7/8"
Y. CEDAR

DECK: 1/4" MAR. PLY

PARTNERS: 3/4" D. FIR

FLOORBOARDS:
3/8"X 3" MAHOG.

9' DE. DINGHY
FOR: SEABREEZ LTD.
DATE: 7-10-89
SCALE: 1 1/2" = 1'-0"
COLD-MOLDED CONS.
LOA: 9'-0"
LWL: 8'-6"
BEAM: 4'-6"
DRAFT: 0'-7"
FREEBOARD
FWD: 1'-7 1/2"
LEAST: 1'-1"
AFT: 1'-5"

JAY R. BENFORD
P.O. BOX 447
ST. MICHAELS, MD 21663
(301) 745-3235

228-4

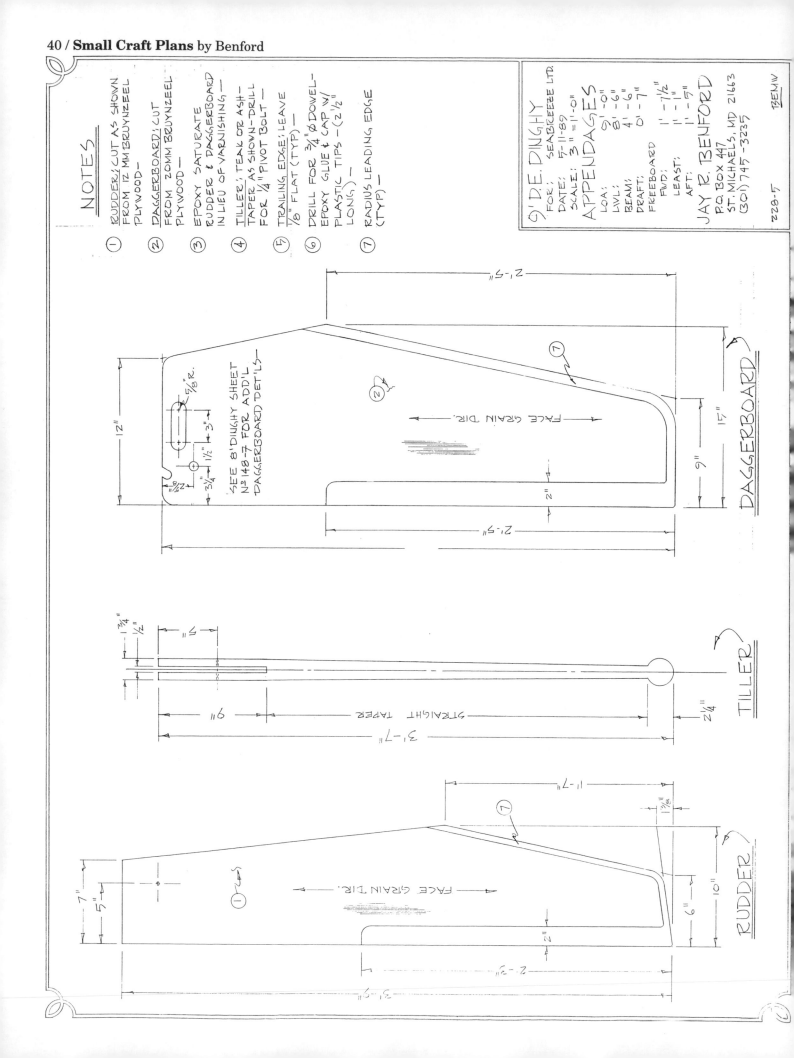

Chapter 7
9 1/2′ Dinghy

This design was done for a firm planning to rotomold the boats in plastic.

Rotomolding is a specialized method of construction. It involves the creation of a metal form of both the outside and inside shape of the boat. Inside these forms are dumped pellets of the special plastic. The form is heated while it is being rotated in two axes at the same time. The heat melts the plastic and it forms itself into the shape of the mold. Most of the boat fenders we see, often made as net floats, are made this way.

I spent quite a lot of time thinking about how the mold was to be built of steel. I came to be increasingly concerned about the work involved in trying to recreate the sweeping shapes of traditional lapstrake wooden plank layout in steel. I felt it would be much too complex a project.

The results of this cogitation was to try the idea of making the laplines all straight lines on the body plan view. This looked good on the drawings, and the work involved in building the molds should be considerably reduced. The layout is much simpler, and the offsets are just given along the laps, as if they were diagonals.

The wooden lapstrake construction shown on the plans is a good way to build the boat. The simplified lap layout and lofting will make fitting the planks much easier and thus quicker.

If a sailing version is desired. I'd use the rig and parts off the 9′ Pacific Peapod design.

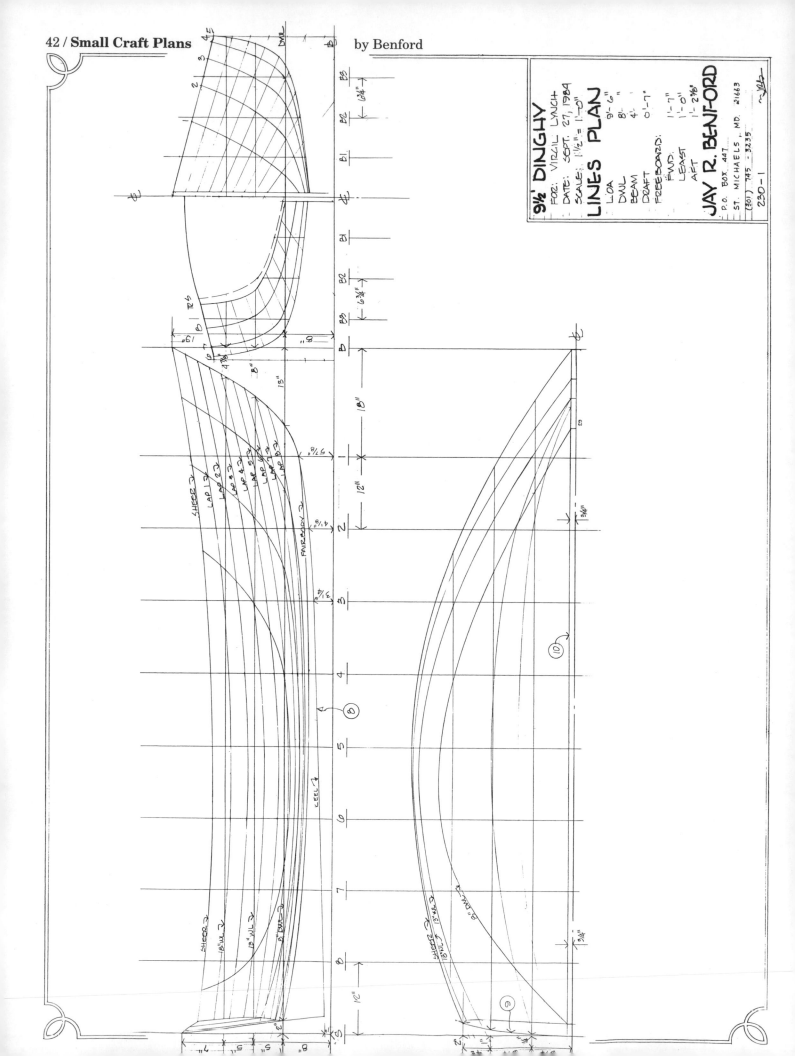

9½' DINGHY

FOR: VIRGIL LYNCH
DATE: SEPT. 27, 1984
SCALE: 1½" = 1'-0"

LINES PLAN

LOA .... 9'-6"
DWL .... 8'-
BEAM .... 4'-
DRAFT .... 0'-7"
FREEBOARD:
    FWD. ...... 1'-7"
    LEAST ..... 1'-0"
    AFT .... 1'-2⅝"

JAY R. BENFORD

P.O. BOX 447
ST. MICHAELS, MD. 21663
(301) 745 - 3235

230 - 1

STATION	TRANSOM	8	7	6	5	4	3	2	1
SHEER	1-6-10	1-10-11	2-1-13	2-3-8	2-3-12	2-2-11	1-11-14	1-7-4	1-1-1
LAP 1	1-6-9	1-10-9	2-1-11	2-3-7	2-3-13	2-2-4	1-11-4	1-6-8	1-0-3
LAP 2	1-6-6	1-10-2	2-1-7	2-3-3	2-3-6	2-1-2	1-10-8	1-5-11	0-11-5
LAP 3	1-5-13	1-9-6	2-0-12	2-2-2	2-2-15	2-0-15	1-9-1	1-4-12	0-10-6
LAP 4	1-4-0	1-7-14	1-11-9	2-1-0	2-1-10	1-11-13	1-8-8	1-3-10	0-9-7
LAP 5	1-1-15	1-5-0	1-9-3	1-10-15	1-11-5	1-9-14	1-7-1	1-2-1	0-8-7
LAP 6	1-1-1	1-2-8	1-5-14	1-7-9	1-7-13	1-6-13	1-4-13	1-1-1	0-7-7
LAP 7	0-11-3	0-11-5	1-2-2	1-3-9	1-3-15	1-3-5	1-1-15	0-11-4	0-6-5
LAP 8	0-8-3	0-7-10	0-9-14	0-11-1	0-11-7	0-11-2	0-10-5	0-8-7	0-5-1
℄ TO FAIRBODY (HEIGHTS)	0-8-0	0-6-2	0-4-14	0-4-4	0-3-14	0-3-15	0-4-3	0-4-11	0-5-11

LOFTING ℄ LAP LAYOUT:

LAP DETAIL: FULL SIZE

KEEL LOFTING DETAIL: HALF SIZE

KEEL HEIGHTS

FAIRBODY 10

9½' DINGHY
FOR: VIRGIL LYNCH
DATE: NOV. 1, 1984
SCALE: 1½"=1'-0"

OFFSETS ℄ NOTES

LOA .... 9'-6"
DWL .... 8'-3"
BEAM .... 4'-6"
DRAFT .... 0'-7"
FREEBOARD:
  FWD .... 1'-7"
  LEAST ...... 1'-0"
  AFT .... 1'-2⅝"

JAY R. BENFORD
P.O. BOX 447
ST. MICHAELS, MD. 21663
(301) 745-3235

NOTES:

1. OFFSETS IN FEET-INCHES-SIXTEENTHS TO OUTSIDE OF HULL. OFFSETS TAKEN ALONG LAPS ON DIAGONALS AS SHOWN, FROM ℄ OUT TO INTERSECTION WITH SHEER OR LAP. (EXCEPT ℄ TO FAIRBODY, WHICH IS A HEIGHT ABOVE ℄.)

2. LAP OFFSETS ARE TO OUTER CORNER OF LAPS. LAPS TO BE 3/8" FULL LENGTH, EXCEPT THAT FORWARD ℄ AFT ENDS TO TAPER OUT OVER 12" TO NO LAPS AT STEM ℄ AT TRANSOM.

3. LINES MUST BE LOFTED ℄ FAIRED FULL SIZE.

4. HALF-SIDING OF STEM ℄ KEEL IS 3/4" — KEEL SIDES FLARE OUTWARDS AS SHOWN IN DETAIL. →

5. THESE PLANS ARE THE PROPERTY OF THE DESIGNER ℄ MAY BE USED ONLY AS AUTHORIZED BY THE DESIGNER IN WRITING.

6. ANY ALTERATION FROM THESE PLANS RELIEVES THE DESIGNER FROM ANY FURTHER RESPONSIBILITY.

7. IT IS UNDERSTOOD THAT NO BOATS WILL BE BUILT FROM THESE PLANS WITHOUT PAYMENT TO THE DESIGNER OF HIS DESIGN ROYALTIES.

8. KEEL IS STRAIGHT LINE IN PROFILE FROM AFT END TO STATION 3, THEN ℄ TO BE TANGENT TO STEM PROFILE BELOW DWL.

9. TRANSOM CURVATURE (DIMENSIONED IN PLAN VIEW) TO APPLY FULL HEIGHT. TRANSOM OFFSETS (ABOVE) ARE INTERSECTIONS WITH THIS CURVED PLANE.

10. FAIRBODY IS 3/4" OFF ℄ — NOTE THAT SLOPED SHEER ℄ LAP LINES ARE DIMENSIONED AT FAIRBODY ℄ CONTINUE THROUGH FAIRBODY TO ℄ — USE ℄ POSITIONS TO CONSTRUCT MIRROR IMAGE LAYOUT FOR OTHER SIDE OF BODY PLAN ℄ ACTUAL BOAT.

11. SHEER ℄ LAP LINES ARE STRAIGHT LINES, LAID OUT AS DIMENSIONED. →

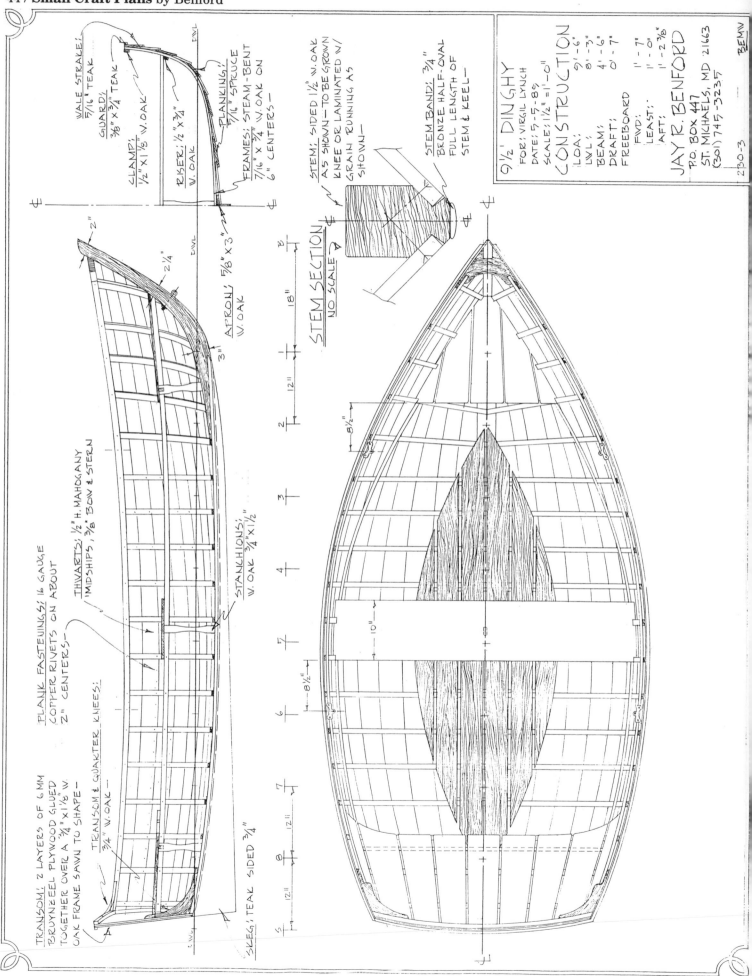

WALE STRAKE; 7/16" TEAK

GUARD; 3/8" x 3/4" TEAK

CLAMP; 1/2" x 1 1/8" W. OAK

PLANKING; 7/16" SPRUCE

RISER; 1/2" x 3/4" W. OAK

FRAMES; STEAM-BENT 7/16" x 3/4" W. OAK ON 6" CENTERS

APRON; 5/8" x 3" W. OAK

STEM; SIDED 1 1/2" W. OAK AS SHOWN—TO BE GROWN KNEE OR LAMINATED W/ GRAIN RUNNING AS SHOWN

STEM BAND; 3/4" BRONZE HALF-OVAL FULL LENGTH OF STEM & KEEL

STEM SECTION
NO SCALE

2"

2 1/4"

3"

B

18"

12"

2

3

4

7

6

7

8

12"

5

LWL

A

PLANK FASTENING; 16 GAUGE COPPER RIVETS ON ABOUT 2" CENTERS

THWARTS; 1/2" H. MAHOGANY MIDSHIPS, 3/8" BOW & STERN

STANCHIONS; W. OAK 3/4" x 1 1/2"

TRANSOM; 2 LAYERS OF 6 MM BROWZEEL PLYWOOD GLUED TOGETHER OVER A 3/4" x 1 1/8" W. OAK FRAME SAWN TO SHAPE

TRANSOM & QUARTER KNEES; 3/4" W. OAK

SKEG; TEAK SIDED 3/4"

8 1/2"

10"

8 1/2"

9 1/2' DINGHY
FOR; VIRGIL LYNCH
DATE; 5-5-89
SCALE; 1 1/2" = 1'-0"
CONSTRUCTION
LOA; 9'-6"
LWL; 8'-3"
BEAM; 4'-6"
DRAFT; 0'-7"
FREEBOARD
    FWD; 1'-7"
    LEAST; 1'-0"
    AFT; 1'-2 3/8"

JAY R. BENFORD
P.O. BOX 447
ST. MICHAELS, MD 21663
(301) 745-3235

230-3

BEMV

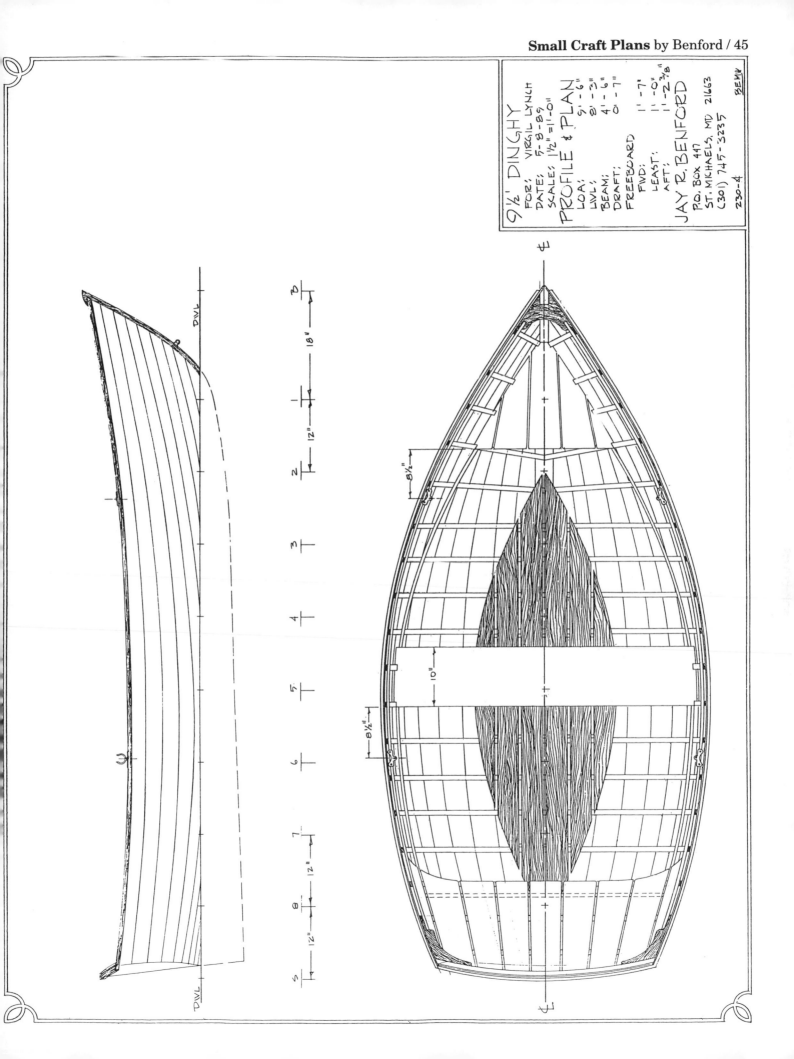

9½' DINGHY
FOR: VIRGIL LYNCH
DATE: 5-8-89
SCALE: 1½"=1'-0"
PROFILE & PLAN
LOA: 9'-6"
LWL: 8'-3"
BEAM: 4'-6"
DRAFT: 0'-7"
FREEBOARD:
    FWD: 1'-7"
    LEAST: 1'-0"
    AFT: 1'-2¾"
JAY R. BENFORD
P.O. BOX 447
ST. MICHAELS, MD 21663
(301) 745-3235

230-4

Chapter 8
11' Oregon Peapod

This design came about when I got to thinking about having an elegant dinghy for our 34' Topsail Ketch SUNRISE. Since she was a double ender (with a pinky stern) I thought it would be fun to have a double ended dinghy.

I showed the idea to the clients for whom we were designing the 8' Portland Yawlboat and another 11-footer. They liked it and decided to go ahead with it instead of the other 11-footer we'd started.

The classic Down East peapod, named in honor of her shape, was most commonly used in lobstering alongshore, where a larger boat could not safely work. The Oregon Peapod has a fuller stern than the Down East style peapod, to give better bearing aft for clamping on an outboard engine.

She is big enough to serve well as a trailered boat, sailed off the beach, or as a car-topper. She can carry a normal family and their picnicing gear for a day of fun and exploring. Or, she can be carried aboard a larger cruising boat as a dinghy or shore boat.

Our arrangement with the builders was that they were to pay us a nominal design fee, and we were to

get dinghies 1, 51, 101, and so forth as our design royalties. I'd be awash in dinghies now if they'd gone ahead with their building program.

However, as I've learned to be an axiom in the marine business, when the builder doesn't want to spend the money to pay for a proper design fee, either through poverty or parsimony, there is very little likelihood of the project ever seeing completion. With little invested with the designer, there is little lost in walking away form the project. If there is a substantial investment made in the design, which is the foundation of the enterprise, then there is more of a committment to go ahead with the venture.

Others have gone ahead and built from this design, as the photos show. We have plans for fiberglass and wood construction, and these are shown on the following pages.

The design calls for two mast steps, allowing her to be sailed as a sloop as shown on the sail plan, or as a catboat. The catboat rig involves moving the mast to the forward position and not using the jib. This could work well as a reefed rig in gustier conditions, or for training work.

Ed Moore's cold-molded Oregon Peapod (above photos) worked out quite nicely.

Mike Kiefer of Great Lakes Boatbuilding Co., South Haven, Michigan, has an Oregon Peapod under construction (below photos) for the designer. He's using glued lapstrake construction to produce a light and rugged sailing dinghy. Photos courtesy of the builders.

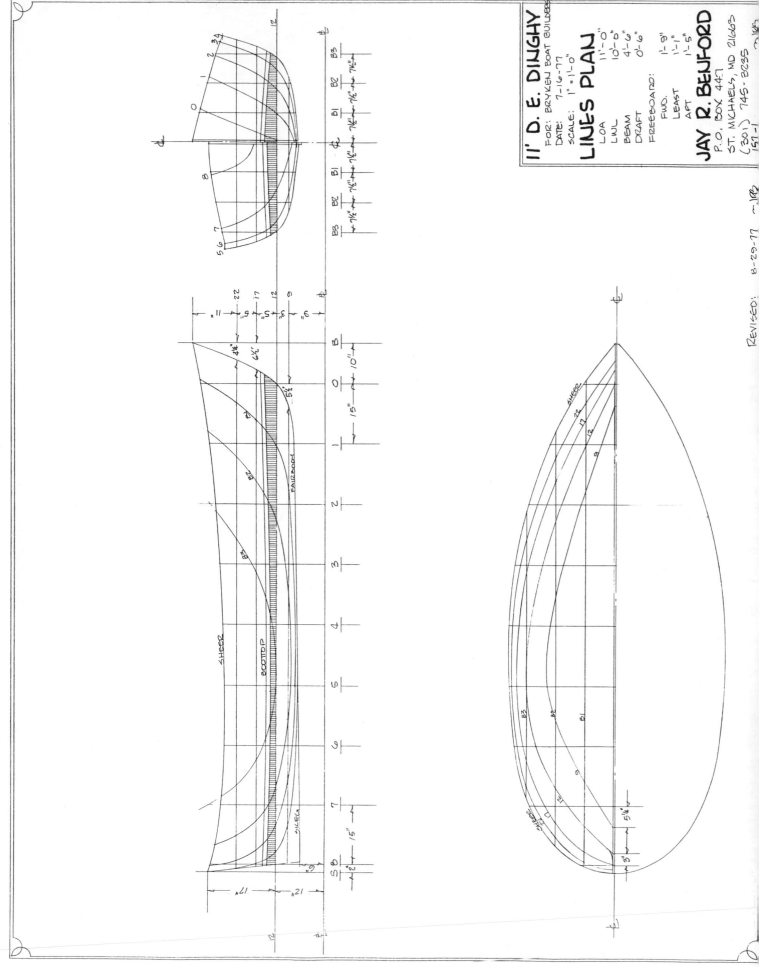

11' D. E. DINGHY

FOR: BRYKEN BOAT BUILDERS
DATE: 7-16-77

LINES PLAN

SCALE: 1" = 1'-0"

LOA   11'-0"
LWL   10'-8"
BEAM   4'-6"
DRAFT   0'-6"

FREEBOARD:
  FWD.   1'-9"
  LEAST   1'-1"
  AFT   1'-5"

JAY R. BENFORD
P.O. BOX 447
ST. MICHAELS, MD 21663
(301) 745-3235
151-1

REVISED: 8-29-77

NOTES:

(1) LINES & OFFSETS IN FEET- INCHES-EIGHTHS. TO OUTSIDE OF HULL. DEDUCT FOR SHELL THICKNESS AS DIRECTED.

(2) LINES MUST BE LOFTED & FAIRED FULL SIZE — DO NOT SCALE PRINTS & OFFSETS.

(3) ANY ALTERATION FROM THESE PLANS RELIEVES THE DESIGNERS FROM ANY FURTHER RESPONSIBILITY.

(4) THESE PLANS ARE THE PROPERTY OF THE DESIGNERS & MAY BE USED ONLY AS AUTHORIZED BY THE DESIGNERS IN WRITING.

(5) IT IS UNDERSTOOD THAT NO MORE THAN ONE BOAT WILL BE BUILT FROM THESE PLANS WITHOUT WRITTEN PERMISSION FROM THE DESIGNERS.

(6) BOOTTOP OFFSETS TO TOP EDGE OF STRIPE. STRIPE IS 1" HIGH IN PROFILE FULL LENGTH.

11' D.E. DINGHY

For: Bayard Boat Builders
Date: Aug. 29, 1977
Scale: As Noted

OFFSETS & NOTES

LOA	11'-0"
LWL	10'-0"
BEAM	4'-6"
DRAFT	0'-6"
FREEBOARD:	
FWD.	1'-9"
LEAST	1'-1"
AFT	1'-5"

JAY R. BENFORD
P.O. BOX 447
ST. MICHAELS, MD. 21663
(301) 745-3235
157-2

STATION	8	7	6	5	4	3	2	1	0
HEIGHTS									
℄ TO FAIRBODY	1-5-5	0-8-1	0-7-1	0-6-5	0-6-7	0-7-1	0-7-3	0-7-5	1-0-0
" B1	2-1-6	0-10-3	0-8-0	0-7-2	0-7-3	0-7-7	0-8-5	1-0-3	2-6-3
" B2	—	—	0-9-7	0-8-3	0-8-4	0-9-7	1-1-5	2-1-6	—
" B3	—	(2-5-1)	1-3-2	1-0-0	1-0-7	1-6-1	(2-4-5)	—	1-4-0
" BOOTTOP	1-3-3	1-2-1	1-2-5	1-2-4	1-2-4	1-2-6	1-3-1	1-3-4	—
" SHEER	2-4-4	2-2-0	1-1-2	2-1-1	2-1-4	2-2-2	2-3-3	2-4-7	2-7-1
HALF-BREADTHS									
℄ TO 9" WL	—	0-3-6	1-0-1	1-6-2	1-4-3	1-1-1	0-8-5	0-3-5	—
" 12"	0-0-4	0-11-6	1-7-7	1-10-4	1-9-4	1-6-3	1-1-4	0-7-3	0-0-4
" 17"	0-0-4	1-5-6	1-11-1	2-0-7	2-0-2	1-10-1	1-5-3	0-10-5	0-2-4
" "22"	0-5-7	1-8-3	2-0-2	2-2-1	2-1-2	1-11-1	1-7-1	1-1-3	0-4-4
" SHEER	0-8-3	1-9-6	2-1-3	2-2-7	2-2-6	2-1-3	1-6-7	1-4-4	0-8-2

SAIL	FOOT	LUFF	LEECH	AREA SQ. FT.	NOTES!
MAIN	6'-3½"	16'-1"	16'-4"	50	SAILS ARE TO BE CONSTRUCTED
JIB	5'-3"	12'-6"	11'-6"	30	OF 3 OZ. DACRON.

11' SAILING DINGHY

FOR: BIRYKEU BOAT BUILDERS
DATE: 8—1—77
SCALE: 3/4" = 1'-0"

SAIL PLAN

LOA 11'-0"
LWL 10'-0"
BEAM 5'-0"
DRAFT:
     BOARD UP 0'-6"
     BOARD DOWN 3'-0"
SAIL AREA 80 SQ. FT.

JAY R. BENFORD

P. O. BOX 447
ST. MICHAELS, MD 21663
(301) 745-3235
157-3

MAIN
50 SQ. FT.

TOTAL
80 SQ. FT.

JIB
30 SQ. FT.

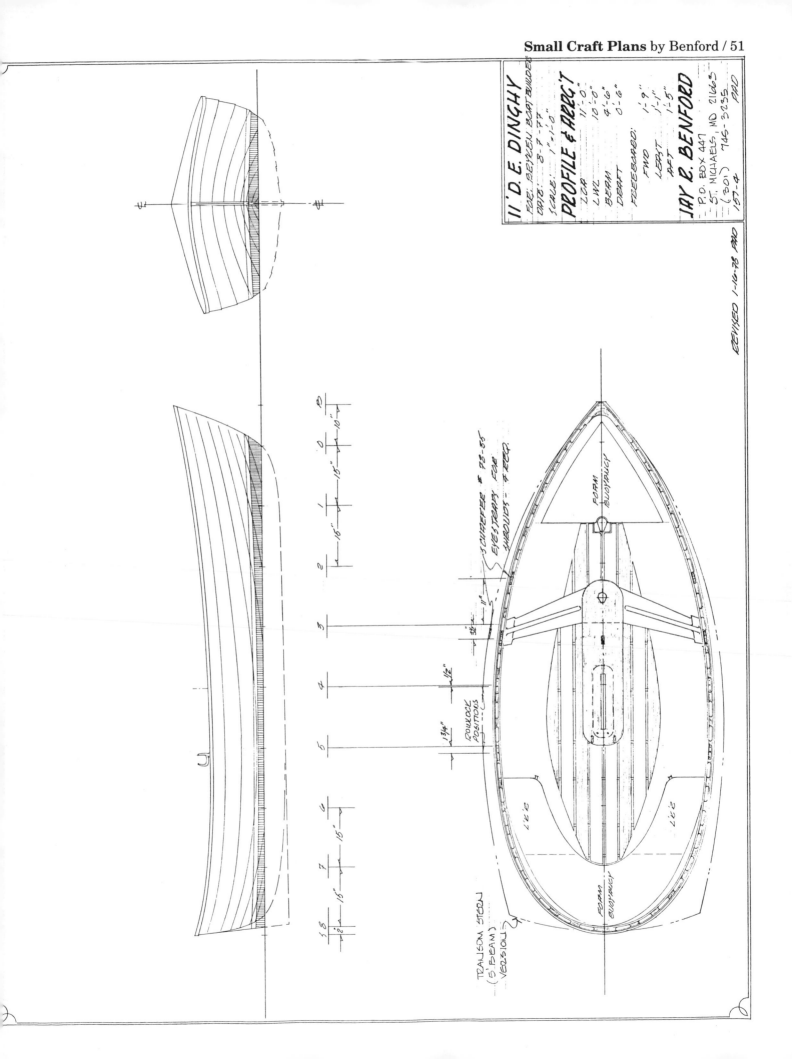

11' D.E. DINGHY

FOR: REVUEN BOAT BUILDERS

DATE: 8-7-77

SCALE: 1"=1'-0"

PROFILE & ARR'C'T

LOA	11'-0"
LWL	10'-0"
BEAM	4'-6"
DRAFT	0'-6"
FREEBOARD:	
FWD	1'-9"
LEAST	1'-1"
AFT	1'-5"

JAY R. BENFORD

P.O. BOX 447
ST. MICHAELS, MD 21663
(301) 745-3235
157-4   PRO

REVISED 1-16-78 PRO

3" CHAMFER # 78-55

EYESTRAPS FOR
SHROUDS = #200

FOAM BUOYANCY

ROWLOCK POSITIONS

TRANSOM STERN
(5' BEAM) VERSION

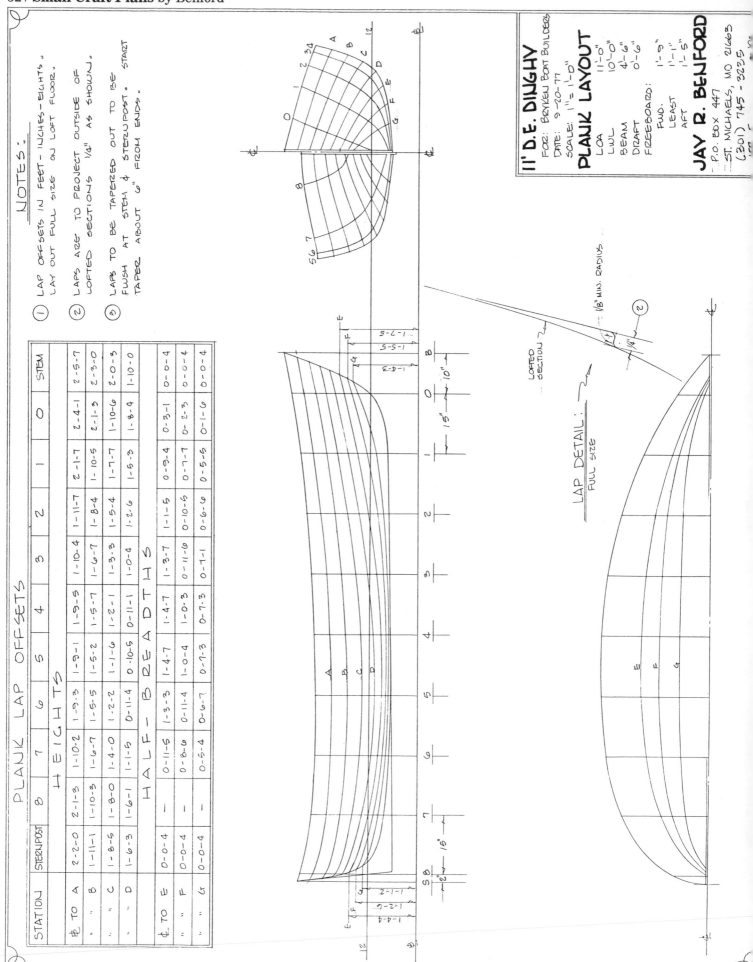

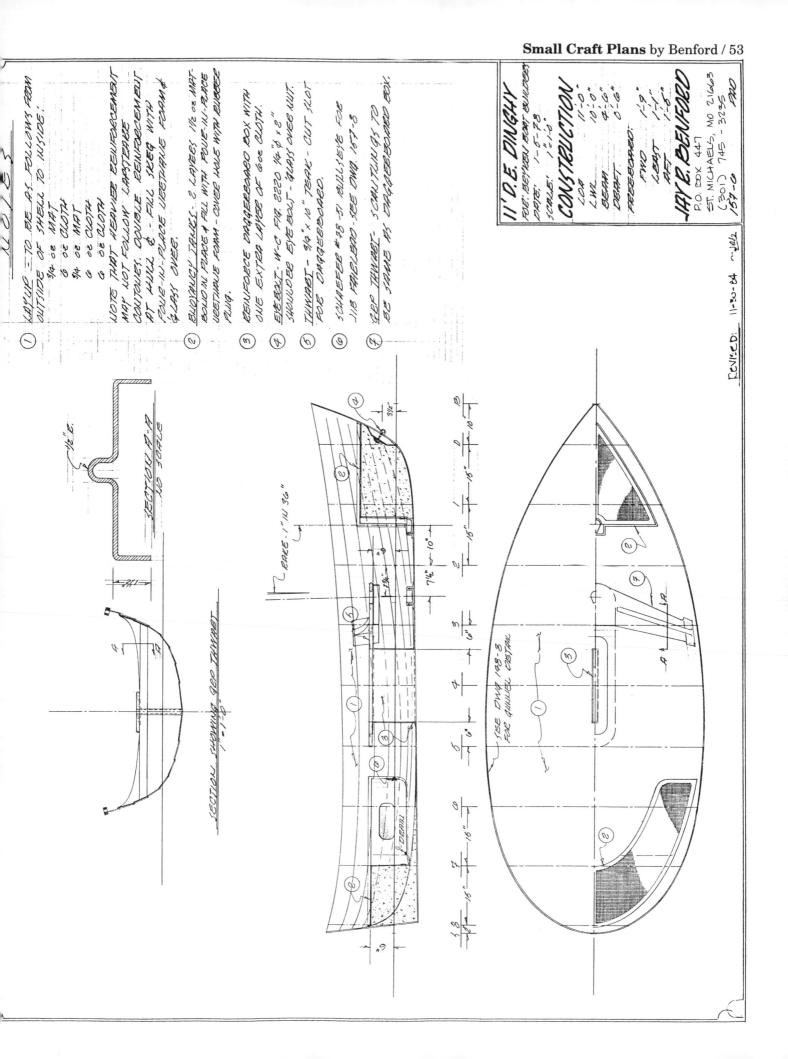

NOTES

1. LAYUP - TO BE AS FOLLOWS FROM OUTSIDE OF SHELL TO INSIDE:
   - 3/4 OZ MAT
   - 6 OZ CLOTH
   - 3/4 OZ MAT
   - 6 OZ CLOTH
   - 6 OZ CLOTH

   NOTE THAT HEAVIER REINFORCEMENT MAY NOT FOLLOW LAPSTRAKE CONTOURS; DOUBLE REINFORCEMENT AT HULL & - FILL SKEG WITH POUR-IN-PLACE URETHANE FOAM & GLASS OVER.

2. BUOYANCY TANKS - 2 LAYERS 1 1/2 OZ MAT - BOND IN PLACE & FILL WITH POUR-IN-PLACE URETHANE FOAM - COVER HOLE WITH RUBBER PLUG.

3. REINFORCE DAGGERBOARD BOX WITH ONE EXTRA LAYER OF 6 OZ CLOTH.

4. EYEBOLT - W-C FIG 2220 1/4"Ø x 2" SHOULDER EYE BOLT - GLASS OVER NUT.

5. THWART - 3/4" x 10" TEAK - CUT SLOT FOR DAGGERBOARD.

6. SCHAEFER #18-51 BULLSEYE FOR JIB FAIRLEAD - SEE DWG 159-8

7. GEP THWART - SCANTLINGS TO BE SAME AS DAGGERBOARD BOX.

SECTION A-A NO SCALE

SECTION SHOWING GEP THWART 1"=1'-0

11' D.E. DINGHY
FOR: BENFORD BOAT BUILDERS
DATE: 1-6-78
SCALES: 1"=1'-0

CONSTRUCTION

LOA	11'-0"
LWL	10'-0"
BEAM	4'-6"
DRAFT	0'-6"

FREEBOARD:
FWD	1'-9"
LEAST	1'-1"
AFT	1'-6"

JAY R. BENFORD
P.O. BOX 447
ST. MICHAELS, MD 21663
(301) 745-3235
159-C

REVISED: 11-30-84

SEE DWG 148-8 FOR GUNWEL DETAIL

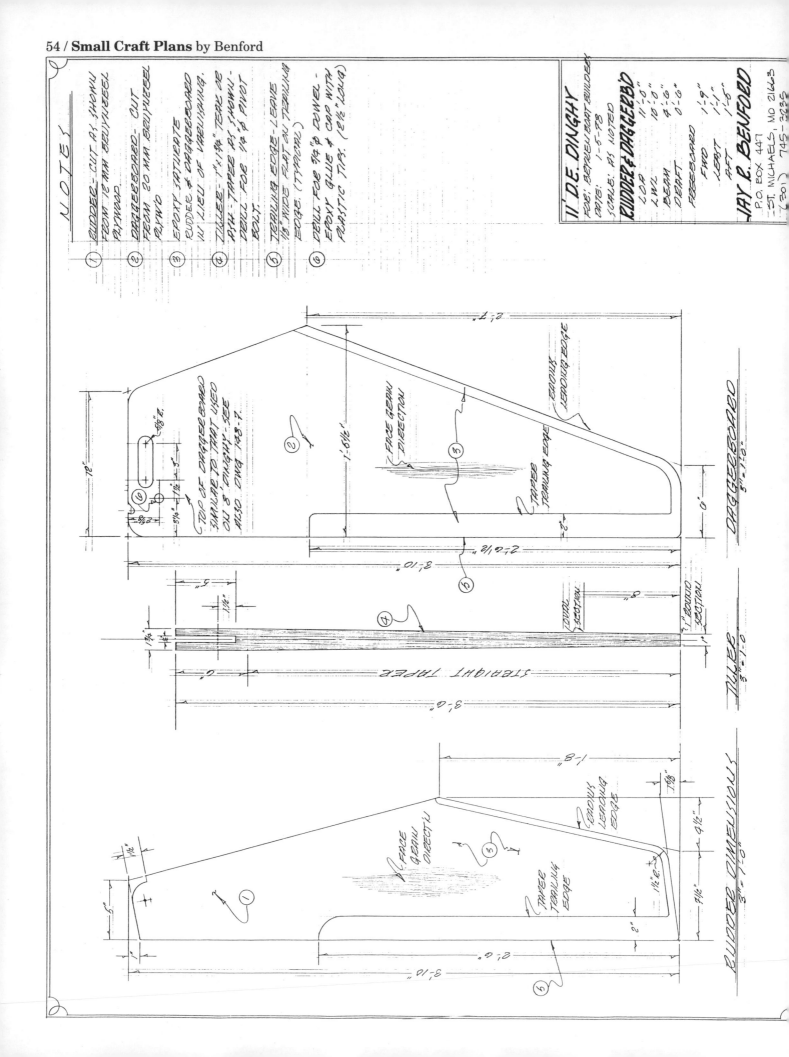

NOTES

1. RUDDER - CUT AS SHOWN FROM 18 MM BRUYNZEEL PLYWD.

2. DAGGERBOARD - CUT FROM 20 MM BRUYNZEEL PLYWD

3. EPOXY SATURATE RUDDER & DAGGERBOARD IN LIEU OF VARNISHING.

4. TILLER 1"x1¾" TEAK AS ASH - TAPER AS SHOWN. DRILL FOR ½"ø PIVOT BOLT.

5. TRAILING EDGE - LEAVE ⅛" WIDE FLAT AT TRAILING EDGE. (TYPICAL)

6. DRILL FOR ¾"ø DOWEL - EPOXY GLUE & CAP WITH PLASTIC TIPS. (2½" LONG)

11' D.E. DINGHY
FOR: BEREU BOAT BUILDERS
DATE: 1-5-78
SCALE: AS NOTED

RUDDER & DAGGERBD

	LOA	11'-0"
	LWL	10'-0"
	BEAM	4'-6"
	DRAFT	0'-6"
FREEBOARD	FWD	1'-9"
	LEAST	1'-1"
	AFT	1'-6"

JAY R. BENFORD
P.O. BOX 447
ST. MICHAELS, MD 21663
(301) 745-3235

DAGGERBOARD
5"=1'-0"

TILLER
3"=1'-0

STRAIGHT TAPER

RUDDER DIMENSIONS
3"=1'-0"

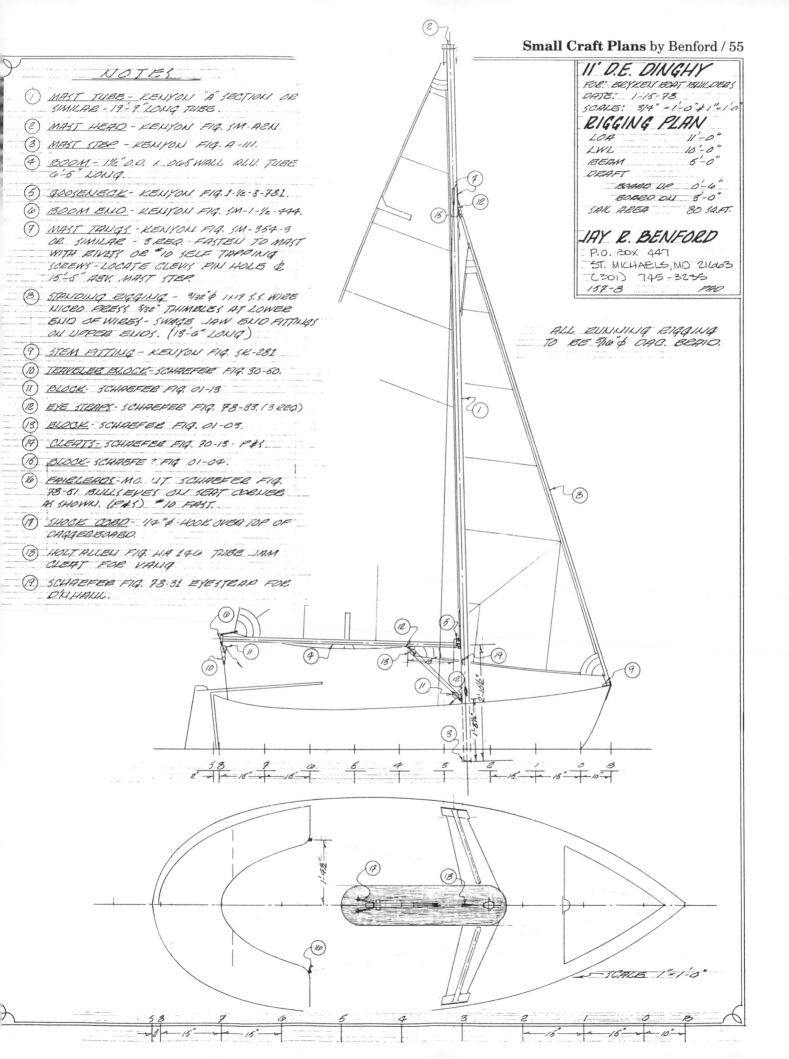

N O T E S

1. MAST TUBE - KENYON "A" SECTION OR SIMILAR - 19'-9" LONG TUBE.
2. MAST HEAD - KENYON FIG. SM-A2N.
3. MAST STEP - KENYON FIG. A-111.
4. BOOM - 1½" O.D. x .065 WALL ALU. TUBE 6'-5" LONG.
5. GOOSENECK - KENYON FIG. 1-1½-3-781.
6. BOOM END - KENYON FIG. SM-1-½-444.
7. MAST TANGS - KENYON FIG. SM-354-8 OR SIMILAR - 3 REQ. FASTEN TO MAST WITH RIVETS OR #10 SELF TAPPING SCREWS - LOCATE CLEVIS PIN HOLE ₵ 15'-5" ABV. MAST STEP.
8. STANDING RIGGING - 3/32"⌀ 1x19 S.S. WIRE NICRO PRESS 3/32" THIMBLES AT LOWER END OF WIRES - SWAGE JAW END FITTINGS ON UPPER ENDS. (13'-6" LONG)
9. STEM FITTING - KENYON FIG. SK-281
10. TRAVELER BLOCK - SCHAEFER FIG. 30-60.
11. BLOCK - SCHAEFER FIG. 01-13
12. EYE STRAPS - SCHAEFER FIG. 78-33. (3 REQ)
13. BLOCK - SCHAEFER FIG. 01-03.
14. CLEATS - SCHAEFER FIG. 70-13 - P&S.
15. BLOCK - SCHAEFER FIG. 01-04.
16. FAIRLEADS - MO. JT SCHAEFER FIG. 78-51 BULLSEYES ON SEAT CORNER AS SHOWN. (P&S) #10 FAST.
17. SHOCK CORD - ¼"⌀ HOOK OVER TOP OF DAGGERBOARD.
18. HOLT ALLEN FIG. HA 140 TUBE JAM CLEAT FOR VANG.
19. SCHAEFER FIG. 78-31 EYESTRAP FOR DWNHAUL.

11' D.E. DINGHY
FOR BRYKEN BOAT BUILDERS
DATE: 1-15-78
SCALE: 3/4"=1'-0" & 1"=1'-0"

RIGGING PLAN
LOA   11'-0"
LWL   10'-0"
BEAM   5'-0"
DRAFT
  BOARD UP   0'-6"
  BOARD DN   3'-0"
SAIL AREA   80 SQ.FT.

JAY R. BENFORD
P.O. BOX 447
ST. MICHAELS, MD 21663
(301) 745-3235
157-8   FIO

ALL RUNNING RIGGING
TO BE 3/16"⌀ DAC. BRAID.

SCALE: 1"=1'-0"

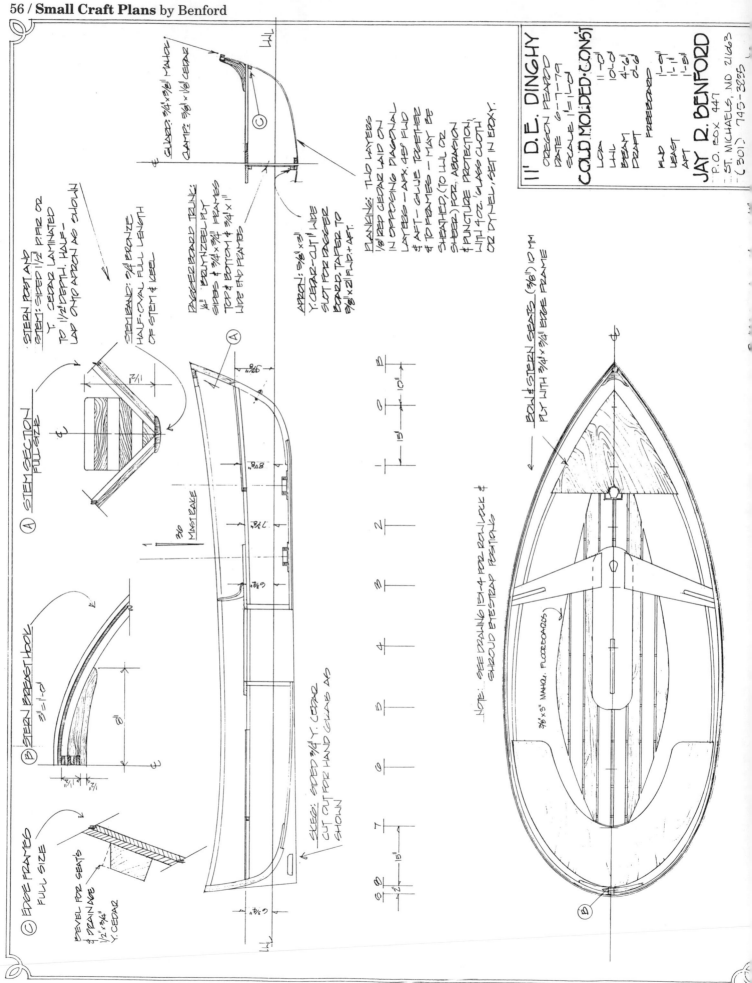

STEM SECTION
FULL SIZE

Ⓐ

STERN POST AND STEM: SIDED 1½" P.FIZ OR Y. CEDAR LAMINATED TO 1½" DEPTH. HALF-LAP ONTO APRON AS SHOWN

STEMBAND: ¾" BRONZE HALF-OVAL FULL LENGTH OF STEM & KEEL.

PLUGGED BOARD TRUNK: ¾" MARINE PLY SIDES & ¾" x ¾" FRAMES TOP & BOTTOM & ¾" x 1½" WIDE END FRAMES

APRON: ⅝" x 3" Y. CEDAR-CUT 1" WIDE SLOT FOR DAGGER BOARD. TAPERED TO ⅝" x 2½" FWD + AFT.

GUARD: ¾" x ⅜" MAHOG. CLAMP: ⅝" x ⅛" CEDAR

Ⓒ

PLANKING: TWO LAYERS ⅛" RED CEDAR LAID ON IN OPPOSING DIAGONAL LAYERS-APX. 45° FWD & AFT-GLUE TOGETHER & TO FRAMES - MAY BE SHEATHED (TO 1½" OZ SHEER) FOR ABRASION & PUNCTURE PROTECTION, WITH 4 OZ. GLASS CLOTH OZ DYNEL, SET IN EPOXY.

STERN BREASTHOOK
3" = 1'-0"

Ⓑ

EDGE FRAMES
FULL SIZE

Ⓒ

BEVEL FOR SEATS & DRAINAGE ½" x ¾" Y. CEDAR

SKEG: SIDED ¾" Y. CEDAR CUT OUT FOR HAND GRIPS AS SHOWN

BOW & STERN SEATS (⅜") PLY WITH ¾" x ¾" EDGE FRAME

NOTE: SEE DRAWING 154-4 FOR ROWLOCK & SHROUD EYESTRAP POSITIONS

⅜" x 3" MAHOG. FLOORBOARDS

Ⓑ

11" D.E. DINGHY
COLD MOLDED·CON5T
OREGON PEAPOD
DATE 6-7-79
SCALE 1"=1'-0

LOA .... 11'-0"
LWL .... 10'-0"
BEAM .... 4'-6"
DRAFT .... 0'-6"

FREEBOARD
MID .... 1'-9"
LEAST .... 1'-1"
AFT .... 1'-5"

JAY R. BENFORD
P.O. BOX 447
ST. MICHAELS, MD 21663
(301) 745-3235

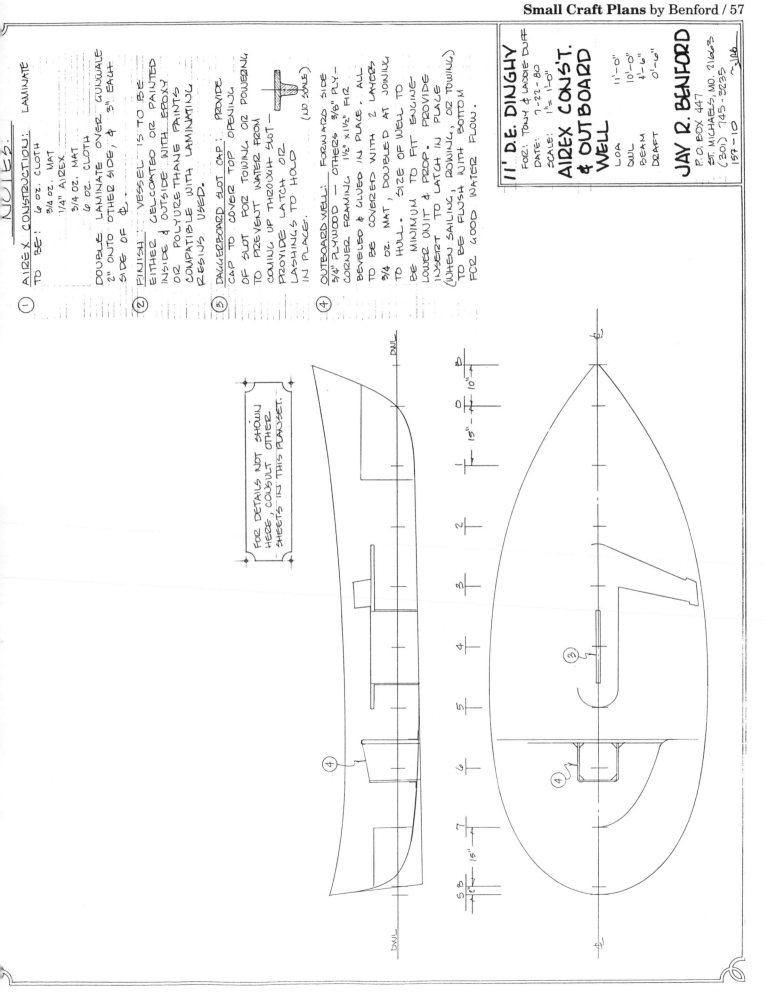

NOTES:

① AIREX CONSTRUCTION: LAMINATE
TO BE: 6 oz. CLOTH
3/4 oz. MAT
1/4" AIREX
3/4 oz. MAT
6 oz. CLOTH

DOUBLE LAMINATE OVER GUNWALE
2" ONTO OTHER SIDE, & 3" EACH
SIDE OF ℄.

② FINISH: VESSEL IS TO BE
EITHER GELCOATED OR PAINTED
INSIDE & OUTSIDE WITH EPOXY
OR POLYURETHANE PAINTS
COMPATIBLE WITH LAMINATING
RESINS USED.

③ DAGGERBOARD SLOT CAP: PROVIDE
CAP TO COVER TOP OPENING
OF SLOT FOR TOWING OR POWERING
TO PREVENT WATER FROM
COMING UP THROUGH SLOT —
PROVIDE LATCH OR
LASHINGS TO HOLD
IN PLACE.

④ OUTBOARD WELL: FORWARD SIDE
3/4" PLYWOOD — OTHERS 3/8" PLY-
CORNER FRAMING 1½" x 1½" FIR
BEVELED & GLUED IN PLACE. ALL
TO BE COVERED WITH 2 LAYERS
3/4 oz. MAT, DOUBLED AT JOINTS
TO HULL. SIZE OF WELL TO
BE MINIMUM TO FIT ENGINE
LOWER UNIT & PROP. PROVIDE
INSERT TO LATCH IN PLACE
(WHEN SAILING, ROWING, OR TOWING)
TO BE FLUSH WITH BOTTOM
FOR GOOD WATER FLOW.

(NO SCALE)

FOR DETAILS NOT SHOWN
HERE, CONSULT OTHER
SHEETS IN THIS PLANSET.

11' D.E. DINGHY
FOR: TONY & LADDIE DUFF
DATE: 7-22-80
SCALE: 1½" = 1'-0"

AIREX CONST.
& OUTBOARD
WELL

LOA   11'-0"
DWL   10'-0"
BEAM   4'-6"
DRAFT   0'-6"

JAY R. BENFORD
P.O. BOX 447
ST. MICHAELS, MD. 21663
(301) 745-3235
157-10

Chapter 9
11′ Dinghy

When we started the design for the Oregon Peapod, we had thought to design a transom stern boat, as a bigger version of the 8′ Portland Yawlboat. They were both commissioned by the same builder, who wanted to have a line of dinghies to sell.

However, as I got further into doing the designs, it occurred to me that we could design a double ender. I did some preliminaries of this and sent them to the clients. They liked the idea, and we went ahead with the double ender instead of the transom stern design.

I saved the drawings for the transom stern version, and later on finished them up for another client to use in building a dinghy for the 50-footer of our design he was building. He reports she is a delightful boat.

All the construction and rigging detailing from the Oregon Peapod would be used for building this version.

Fred Brunhouse's nice cold-molded 11′ dinghy ready to go sailing. She'll stow handily on the flush deck of the 50′ double-ended ketch. The mast will stow vertically along the shrouds. Photo courtesy of the builder.

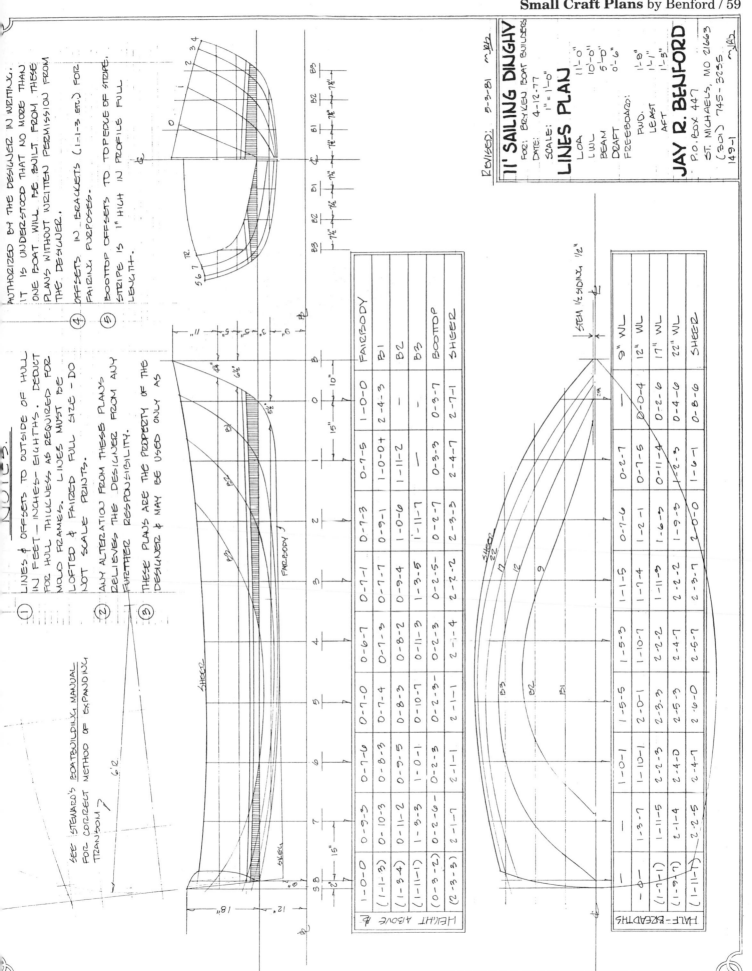

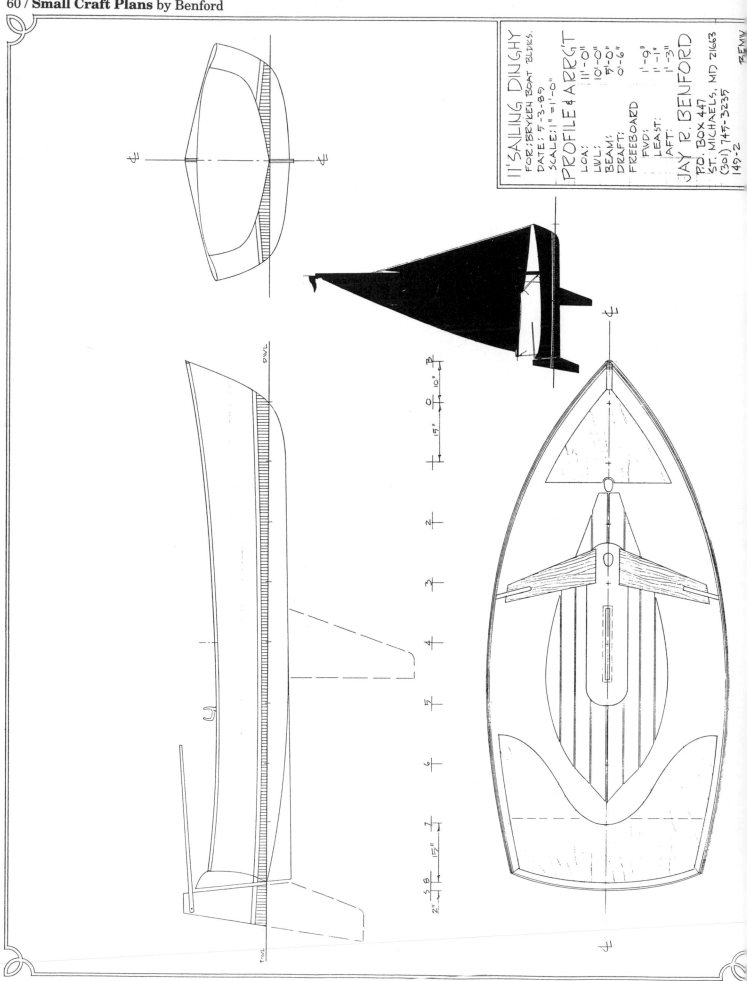

11' SAILING DINGHY
FOR: BRYLEN BOAT BLDRS.
DATE: 5-3-89
SCALE: 1" = 1'-0"

PROFILE & ARR'G'T

LOA: 11'-0"
LWL: 10'-0"
BEAM: 5'-0"
DRAFT: 0'-6"
FREEBOARD
  FWD: 1'-9"
  LEAST: 1'-1"
  AFT: 1'-3"

JAY R. BENFORD
P.O. BOX 447
ST. MICHAELS, MD 21663
(301) 745-3235
149-2

Chapter 10
11′ Dinghy NIGHT

This dinghy was designed for a friend of ours, to serve as tender to his 33′ schooner. He is a marine writer, with a taste for bad puns. He wanted to build the boat, and write an article about the project. "NIGHT is the tender" was to be the title of the article...

The design concept was for a simply built marine plywood dinghy, that had a traditional appearance and spritsail rig. We looked at the possibility of making the bow section removable, using the stern as a pram, and letting the two nest and stow in a smaller space on deck. This is possible to do, although not shown on the drawings.

Her hull form is slender enough to be easily rowed, so she'll be a good pulling boat. This slenderness also means she's easily driven under sail, and the rig should be of generous size for her.

The daggerboard slot is off center, to allow for the large combination box and seat on centerline. The box is to function as storage for the outboard engine and the miscellaneous collection of things that were wanted to be carried along. On a passage, it might have the lifeboat stores and equipment in it.

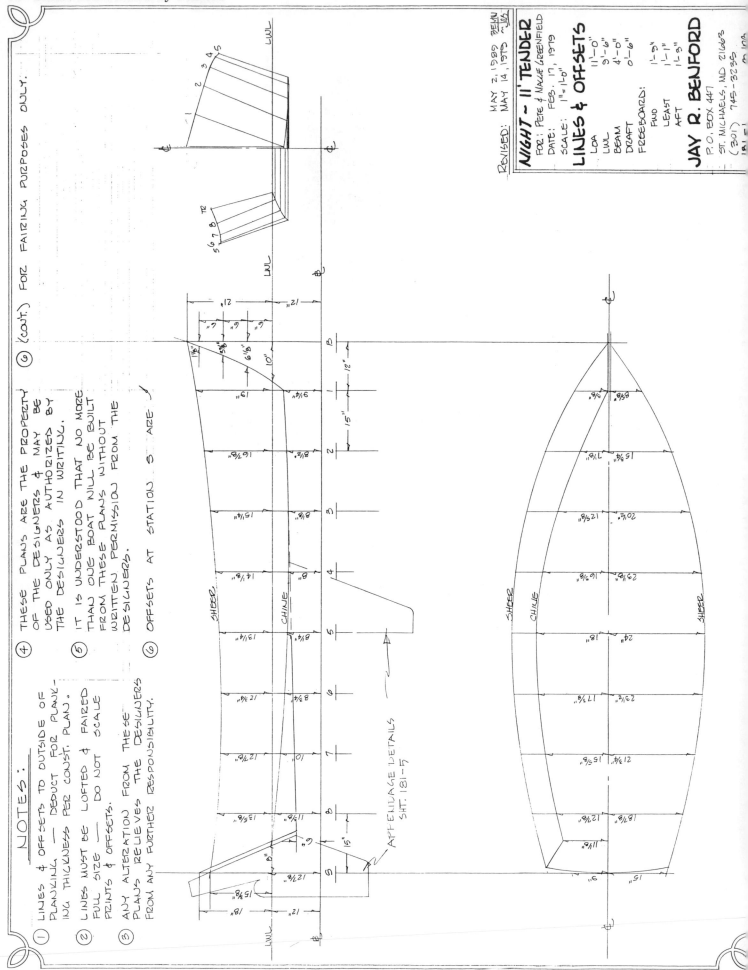

NOTES:

(1) LINES & OFFSETS TO OUTSIDE OF PLANKING. — DEDUCT FOR PLANKING THICKNESS PER CONST. PLAN.

(2) LINES MUST BE LOFTED & FAIRED FULL SIZE — DO NOT SCALE PRINTS & OFFSETS.

(3) ANY ALTERATION FROM THESE PLANS RELIEVES THE DESIGNERS FROM ANY FURTHER RESPONSIBILITY.

(4) THESE PLANS ARE THE PROPERTY OF THE DESIGNERS & MAY BE USED ONLY AS AUTHORIZED BY THE DESIGNERS IN WRITING.

(5) IT IS UNDERSTOOD THAT NO MORE THAN ONE BOAT WILL BE BUILT FROM THESE PLANS WITHOUT WRITTEN PERMISSION FROM THE DESIGNERS.

(6) OFFSETS AT STATION 5 ARE ✓

(6) (CONT.) FOR FAIRING PURPOSES ONLY.

NIGHT ~ 11' TENDER

FOR: PETE & MALLIE GREENFIELD

DATE: FEB. 17, 1979

SCALE: 1" = 1'-0"

REVISED: MAY 2, 1989
MAY 14, 1975

LINES & OFFSETS

LOA	11'-0"
LWL	9'-6"
BEAM	4'-0"
DRAFT	0'-6"
FREEBOARD:	
FWD	1'-5"
LEAST	1'-1"
AFT	1'-3"

JAY R. BENFORD

P.O. BOX 447
ST. MICHAELS, MD. 21663
(301) 745-3235

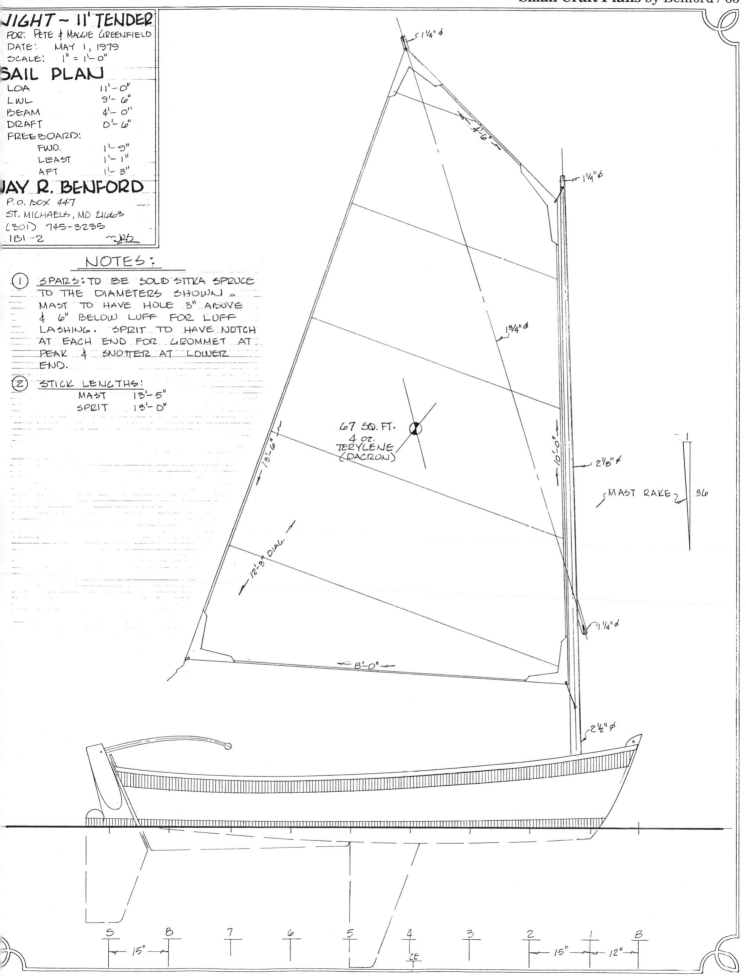

NIGHT ~ 11' TENDER
FOR: PETE & MALLIE GREENFIELD
DATE: MAY 1, 1979
SCALE: 1" = 1'-0"

SAIL PLAN

LOA	11'-0"
LWL	9'-6"
BEAM	4'-0"
DRAFT	0'-6"
FREEBOARD:	
FWD.	1'-9"
LEAST	1'-1"
AFT	1'-3"

JAY R. BENFORD
P.O. BOX 447
ST. MICHAELS, MD 21663
(301) 745-3235
181-2

NOTES:

(1) SPARS: TO BE SOLID SITKA SPRUCE
TO THE DIAMETERS SHOWN. MAST TO HAVE HOLE 3" ABOVE & 6" BELOW LUFF FOR LUFF LASHING. SPRIT TO HAVE NOTCH AT EACH END FOR GROMMET AT PEAK & SNOTTER AT LOWER END.

(2) STICK LENGTHS:
MAST 13'-5"
SPRIT 13'-0"

5 1¼" ⌀

1¼" ⌀

4'-6"

1¾" ⌀

67 SQ. FT.
4 OZ.
TERYLENE
(DACRON)

13'-6"

12'-3" DIAG.

8'-0"

10'-0"

2⅛" ⌀

MAST RAKE 36

1¼" ⌀

2½" ⌀

CE

5   8   7   6   5   4   3   2   1   B
15"   15"   12"

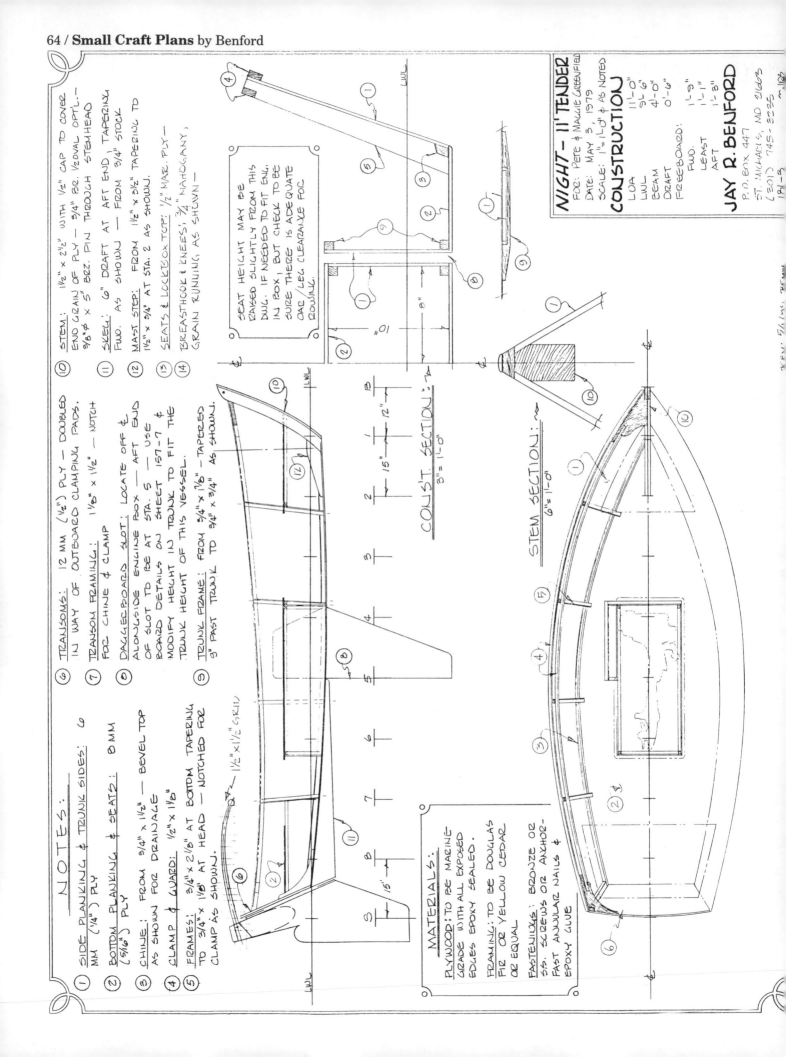

NIGHT – 11' TENDER

FOR: PETE & MAGGIE GREENFIELD
DATE: MAY 3, 1979
SCALE: 1"=1'-0" & AS NOTED

CONSTRUCTION

LOA	11'-0"
LWL	9'-6"
BEAM	4'-0"
DRAFT	0'-0"
FREEBOARD:	
FWD.	1'-9"
LEAST	1'-1"
AFT	1'-8"

JAY R. BENFORD

P.O. BOX 447
ST. MICHAELS, MD 21663
(301) 745-3235

181-3

CONST. SECTION:
3"=1'-0"

STEM SECTION:
6"=1'-0"

SEAT HEIGHT MAY BE
RAISED SLIGHTLY FROM THIS
DWG. IF NEEDED TO FIT ENG.
IN BOX, BUT CHECK TO BE
SURE THERE IS ADEQUATE
OAR/LEG CLEARANCE FOR
ROWING.

NOTES:

1. SIDE PLANKING & TRUNK SIDES: 6 MM (¼") PLY

2. BOTTOM PLANKING & SEATS: 8 MM (5/16") PLY

3. CHINE: FROM ¾" × 1½" — BEVEL TOP AS SHOWN FOR DRAINAGE

4. CLAMP & GUARD: ½" × 1⅛"

5. FRAMES: ¾" × 2⅛" AT BOTTOM TAPERING TO ¾" × 1⅛" AT HEAD — NOTCHED FOR CLAMP AS SHOWN.

6. TRANSOMS: 12 MM (½") PLY — DOUBLED IN WAY OF OUTBOARD CLAMPING PADS.

7. TRANSOM FRAMING: 1⅛" × 1½" — NOTCH FOR CHINE & CLAMP

8. DAGGERBOARD SLOT: LOCATE OFF ℄ ALONGSIDE ENGINE BOX — AFT END OF SLOT TO BE AT STA. 5 — USE BOARD DETAILS ON SHEET 157-7 & MODIFY HEIGHT IN TRUNK TO FIT THE TRUNK HEIGHT OF THIS VESSEL.

9. TRUNK FRAME: FROM ¾" × 1⅛" — TAPERED 3" PAST TRUNK TO ⅜" × ¾" AS SHOWN.

10. STEM: 1½" × 2½" WITH ½" CAP TO COVER END GRAIN OF PLY — ¾" BR. ½ OVAL OPTL — ⅜"ø × 5" BRZ. PIN THROUGH STEMHEAD

11. SKEG: 6" DRAFT AT AFT END, TAPERING FWD. AS SHOWN — FROM ¾" STOCK

12. MAST STEP: FROM 1½" × 5½" TAPERING TO 1½" × ¾" AT STA. 2 AS SHOWN.

13. SEATS & LOCKBOX TOP: ½" MAR. PLY —

14. BREASTHOOK & KNEES: ¾" MAHOGANY, GRAIN RUNNING AS SHOWN —

MATERIALS:

PLYWOOD: TO BE MARINE GRADE WITH ALL EXPOSED EDGES EPOXY SEALED.

FRAMING: TO BE DOUGLAS FIR OR YELLOW CEDAR OR EQUAL

FASTENINGS: BRONZE OR SS. SCREWS OR ANCHORFAST ANNULAR NAILS & EPOXY GLUE

1½" × 1½" GRID

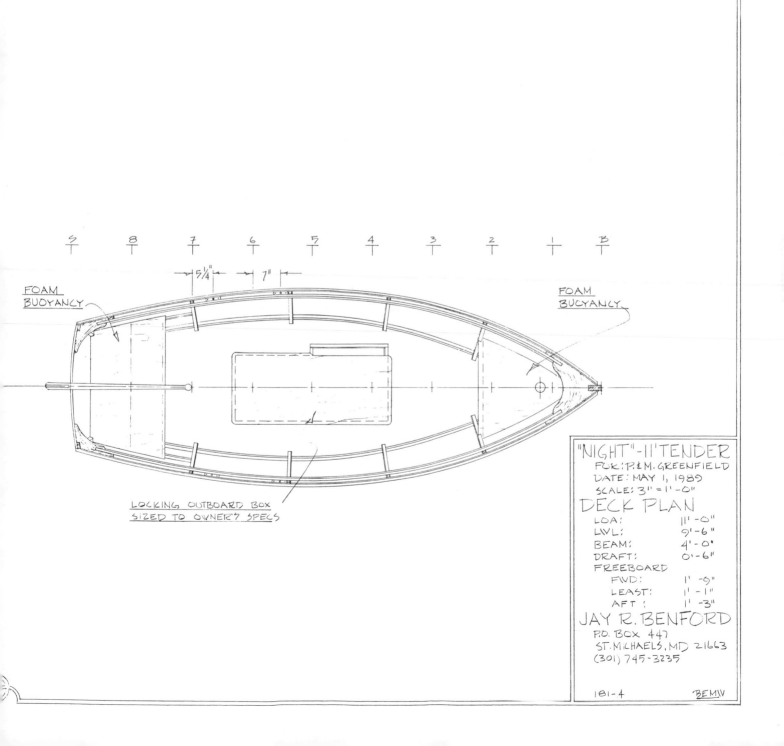

FOAM
BUOYANCY

FOAM
BUOYANCY

LOCKING OUTBOARD BOX
SIZED TO OWNER'S SPECS

"NIGHT"-11'TENDER
FOR: P.&M. GREENFIELD
DATE: MAY 1, 1989
SCALE: 3"=1'-0"
DECK PLAN
LOA: 11'-0"
LWL: 9'-6"
BEAM: 4'-0"
DRAFT: 0'-6"
FREEBOARD
  FWD: 1'-9"
  LEAST: 1'-1"
  AFT: 1'-3"
JAY R. BENFORD
P.O. BOX 447
ST. MICHAELS, MD 21663
(301) 745-3235

181-4   BEMIV

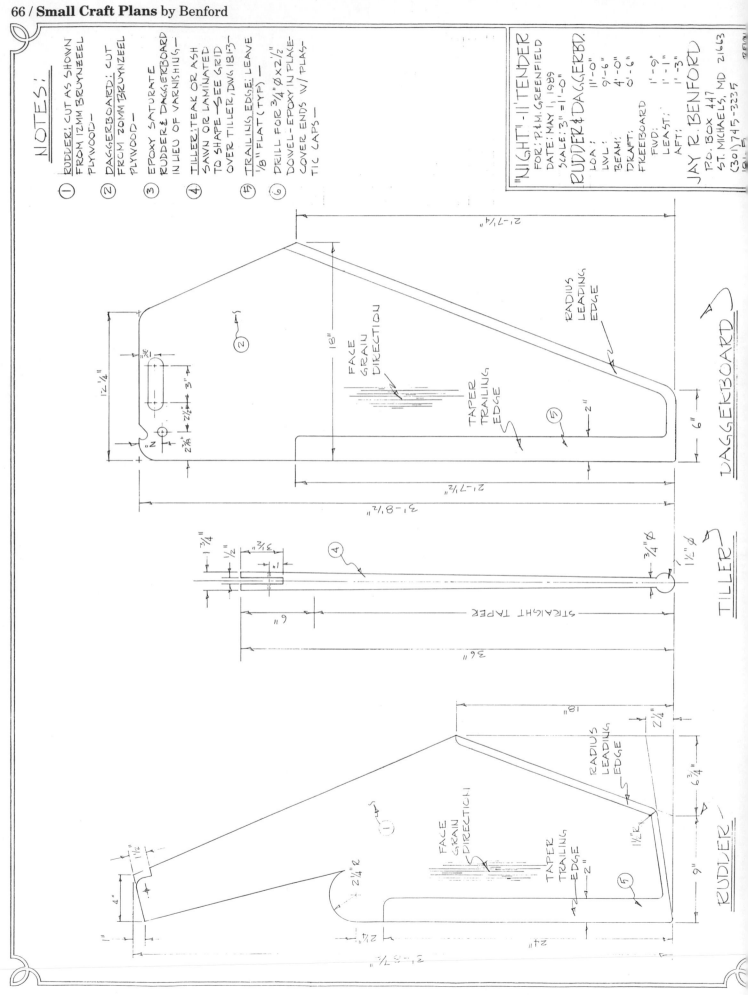

NOTES:

1. RUDDER: CUT AS SHOWN FROM 12MM BRUYNZEEL PLYWOOD—
2. DAGGERBOARD: CUT FROM 20MM BRUYNZEEL PLYWOOD—
3. EPOXY SATURATE RUDDER & DAGGERBOARD IN LIEU OF VARNISHING—
4. TILLER: TEAK OR ASH SAWN OR LAMINATED TO SHAPE—SEE GRID OVER TILLER, DWG 1813—
5. TRAILING EDGE: LEAVE 1/8" FLAT (TYP)—
6. DRILL FOR 3/4"∅ x 2 1/2" DOWEL-EPOXY IN PLACE-COVER ENDS W/ PLASTIC CAPS—

"NIGHT"-11' TENDER
FOR: P&M. GREENFIELD
DATE: MAY 1, 1989
SCALE: 3" = 1'-0"

RUDDER & DAGGERBD.

LOA : 11'-0"
LWL : 9'-6"
BEAM: 4'-0"
DRAFT: 0'-6"
FREEBOARD:
  FWD: 1'-9"
  LEAST: 1'-1"
  AFT: 1'-3"

JAY R. BENFORD
P.O. BOX 447
ST. MICHAELS, MD 21663
(301)745-3235

DAGGERBOARD

TILLER

RUDDER

Chapter 11
11'-4" Dinghy

During the decade that I lived aboard SUNRISE, we tried several different sorts of boats as dinghies and shoreboats. Originally, we had a used, plywood Penquin and added padding around her sheerline to make it easier to lay her alongside our bright finished hull.

After the transom on the Penquin rotted out, we got an Avon 9 1/2' inflatable. This was a great success in not scratching the finish on SUNRISE, and worked excellently as a painting float too. However, as a pulling boat it had the inflatable's usual shortcomings.

After putting up with the inflatable for a few years, I got to thinking more seriously about a good hard dinghy for the longer rowing runs to shore. About this time, a couple friends started building a few of Phil Bolger's Light Dories for sale. I'd always admired them, but felt that they were just too long to carry on the trunk cabin. I'd already decided that I did not want to tow a tender, particularly when I had this excellent place to carry one on the housetop.

So, I took what I thought was the philosophy of simplicity of the Light Dory and drew up this shorter, truncated boat which would just fit on SUNRISE'S housetop. I reckoned that 12' plywood would do for her sides and 10' for the bottom.

When it came time that spring to build her, I was faced with the decision of whether to spend the money on building the dinghy or using that same money to finance a longer summer cruising session.

So,...I had a nice long cruise that summer and never did get to try out the dinghy. The local builders got into something more profitable and I kept using the Avon.

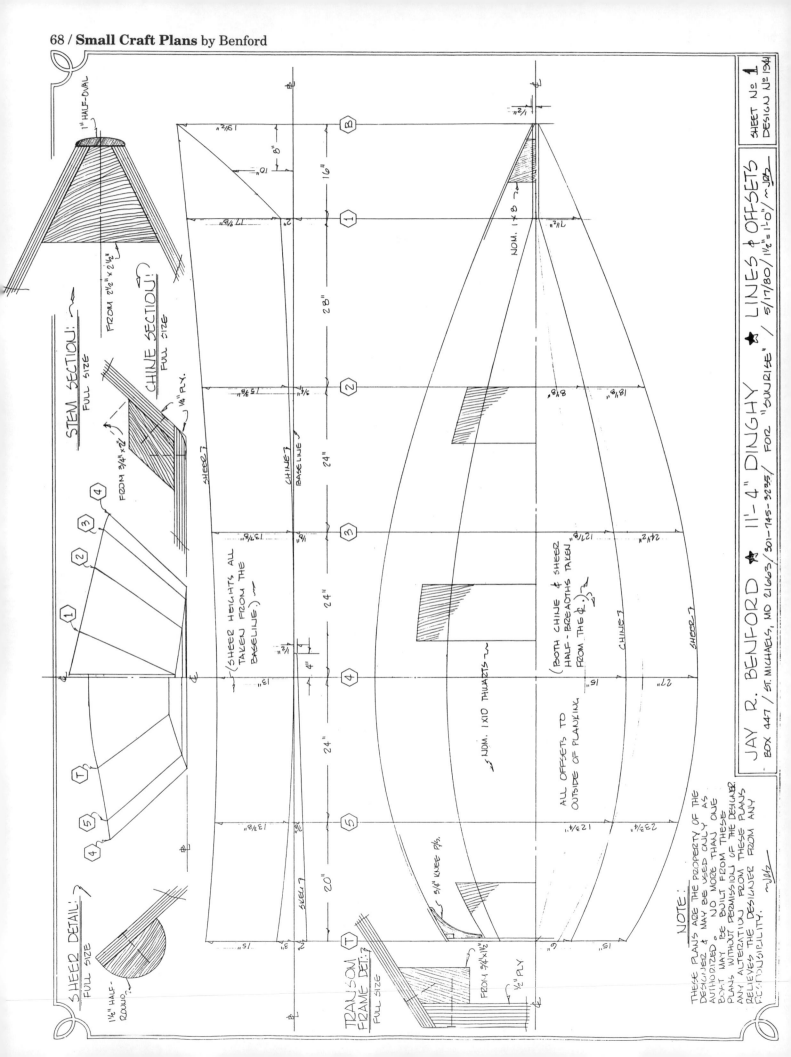

STEM SECTION:
FULL SIZE

CHINE SECTION:
FULL SIZE

SHEER DETAIL:
FULL SIZE

TRANSOM FRAME DET.:
FULL SIZE

JAY R. BENFORD ★ 11'-4" DINGHY ★ LINES & OFFSETS

BOX 447 / ST. MICHAELS, MD 21663/ 301-745-3235/ FOR "SUNRISE" / 5/17/80/ 11½"=1'-0" ~JPS

SHEET № 1
DESIGN № 194

NOTE:
THESE PLANS ARE THE PROPERTY OF THE DESIGNER & MAY BE USED ONLY AS AUTHORIZED & NO MORE THAN ONE BOAT MAY BE BUILT FROM THESE PLANS WITHOUT PERMISSION OF THE DESIGNER. ANY ALTERATION FROM THESE PLANS RELIEVES THE DESIGNER FROM ANY RESPONSIBILITY.

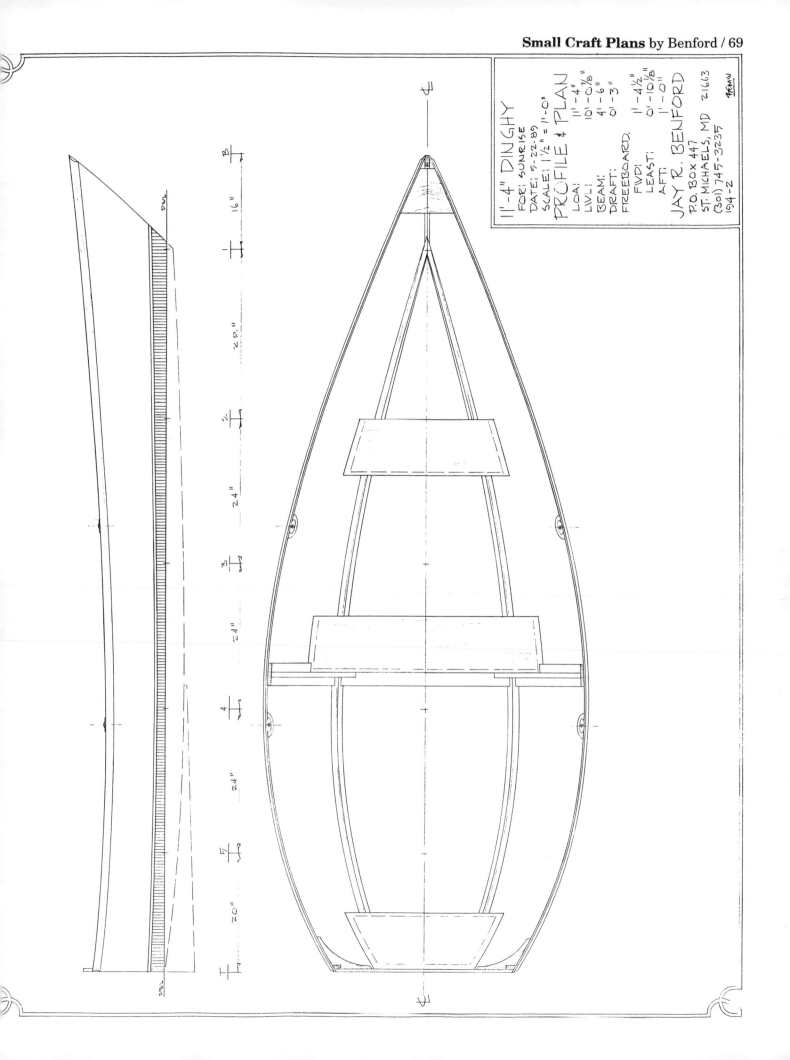

11'-4" DINGHY
FOR: SUNRISE
DATE: 7-22-89
SCALE: 1½" = 1'-0"
PROFILE & PLAN

LOA: 11'-4"
LWL: 10'-0⅞"
BEAM: 4'-6"
DRAFT: 0'-3"
FREEBOARD:
  FWD: 1'-4½"
  LEAST: 0'-10⅛"
  AFT: 1'-0"

JAY R. BENFORD
P.O. BOX 447
ST. MICHAELS, MD 21663
(301) 745-3235
194-2

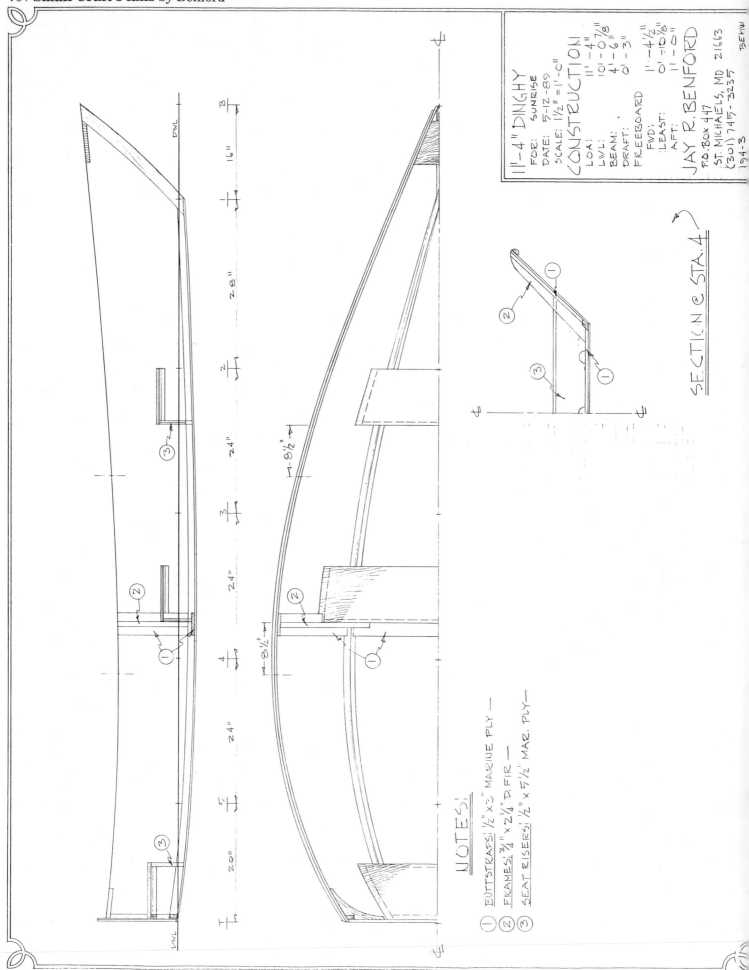

NOTES:

① BUTTSTRAPS: ½" x 3" MARINE PLY —
② FRAMES: ¾" x 2¼" D. FIR —
③ SEAT RISERS: ½" x 5½" MAR. PLY —

SECTION @ STA. 4

11'-4" DINGHY

FOR: SUNRISE
DATE: 5-12-89
SCALE: 1½" = 1'-0"

CONSTRUCTION

LOA: 11' - 4"
LWL: 10' - 0 7/8"
BEAM: 4' - 6"
DRAFT: 0' - 3"
FREEBOARD
   FWD: 1' - 4½"
   LEAST: 0' - 10⅛"
   AFT: 0' - 0"

JAY R. BENFORD
P.O. BOX 447
ST. MICHAELS, MD 21663
(301) 745-3235

194-3

Chapter 12   12′ Keelboat

Back in the early '70's, when it was socially acceptable to be designing in ferro-cement, we did a number of designs in that medium. All the ones done under our supervision and with our techniques and methodology turned out quite well, with such a nice finish on them they were usually taken for nicely built wood boats.

Then, within a few years, the results of Samson Marine's marketing caught up with even the good ones, ruining the resale value for one and all. You see, they had claimed that anyone could build in the medium and do it quickly and cheaply. Unfortunately, the results looked like they had been taken literally. Crude finish work and detailing abounded, and they were difficult to resell for even the cost of their materials. The boating community at large assumed that anything that was built of ferro-cement must, by definition, be one of these crudely built boats and didn't want to be associated with them.

We'd always been doing designs in other materials, and those other materials are what we're working in today. We still sell the occasional ferro-cement plan (almost always overseas), but I won't do it without making my concerns about the resale situation known.

This 12′ Keelboat was designed while we were heavily involved in doing ferro-cement designs and was part of an ongoing materials testing and design evolution program. Samson had claimed that building under 30′ was not practical, but we'd already done a 17′ Catboat. The data we'd gotten from the test lab work proved correct in the success of this boat too.

Living in the Pacific Northwest at the time, most areas had no concerns about draft. We thought we'd try out the idea of a

small keelboat that would be a good performer. The shell thickness was well under 1/4" and she was quite flexible without the gunwale reinforcement.

Today, I think something like this ought to be cold-molded, and the structural detailing of the 11′ Oregon Peapod might work well for her. Living on the shores of the Chesapeake now, I appreciate more of the virtues of shallow draft, and would think about a centerboard or daggerboard too.

When he came to work with us, Peter Dunsford looked at her design and thought she would make the basis for a great little sandbagger. The silhouette below is the results of his sketching on an alternate rig of her.

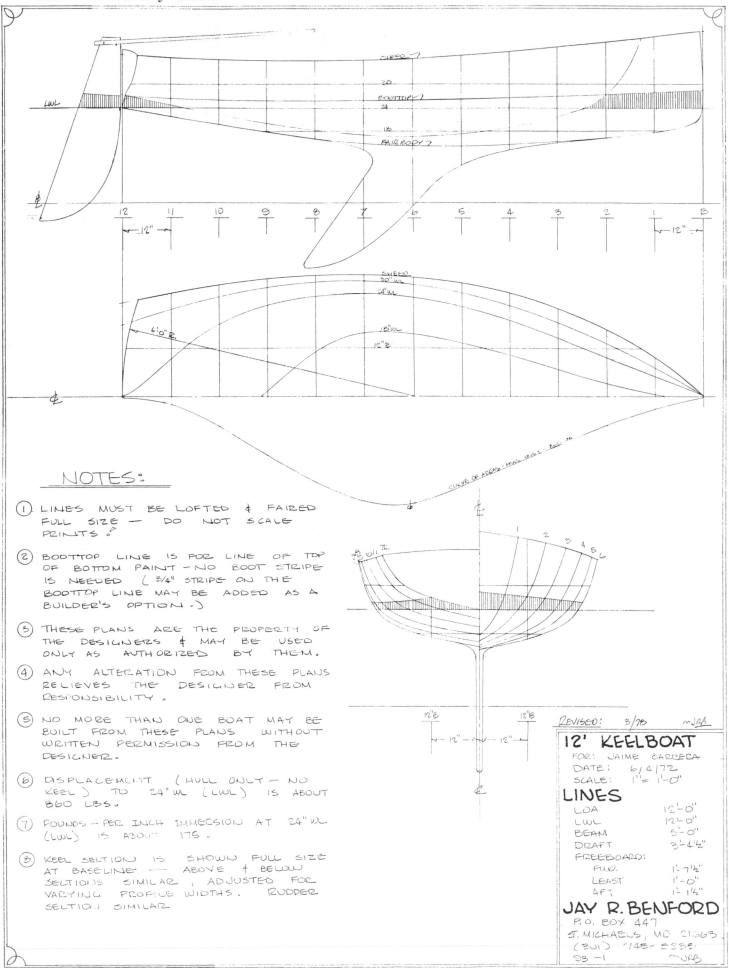

NOTES:

1. LINES MUST BE LOFTED & FAIRED FULL SIZE — DO NOT SCALE PRINTS.

2. BOOTTOP LINE IS FOR LINE OF TOP OF BOTTOM PAINT — NO BOOT STRIPE IS NEEDED (3/4" STRIPE ON THE BOOTTOP LINE MAY BE ADDED AS A BUILDER'S OPTION.)

3. THESE PLANS ARE THE PROPERTY OF THE DESIGNERS & MAY BE USED ONLY AS AUTHORIZED BY THEM.

4. ANY ALTERATION FROM THESE PLANS RELIEVES THE DESIGNER FROM RESPONSIBILITY.

5. NO MORE THAN ONE BOAT MAY BE BUILT FROM THESE PLANS WITHOUT WRITTEN PERMISSION FROM THE DESIGNER.

6. DISPLACEMENT (HULL ONLY — NO KEEL) TO 24" WL (LWL) IS ABOUT 860 LBS.

7. POUNDS — PER INCH IMMERSION AT 24" WL (LWL) IS ABOUT 175.

8. KEEL SECTION IS SHOWN FULL SIZE AT BASELINE — ABOVE & BELOW SECTIONS SIMILAR, ADJUSTED FOR VARYING PROFILE WIDTHS. RUDDER SECTION SIMILAR

REVISED: 3/78

12' KEELBOAT
FOR: JAIME BARCERA
DATE: 6/4/72
SCALE: 1" = 1'-0"

LINES
LOA   12'-0"
LWL   12'-0"
BEAM   5'-0"
DRAFT   3'-4½"
FREEBOARD:
    FWD.   1'-7½"
    LEAST   1'-0"
    AFT   1'-1¼"

JAY R. BENFORD
P.O. BOX 447
ST. MICHAELS, MD 21663
(301) 745-5235
93-1

12' KEELBOAT

FOR: JAIME BARRERA
DATE: MARCH 30 - 1978
SCALE: 1" = 1'-0"

TABLE OF OFFSETS

L.O.A	12'-0"
LWL	12'-0"
BEAM	5'-0"
DRAFT	3'-4½"
FREEBOARD:	
FWD.	1'-7½"
LEAST	1'-0"
AFT.	1'-1½"

JAY R. BENFORD
P.O. BOX 447
ST. MICHAELS, MD 21663
(301) 745-3235

93-3

STATION	12	11	10	9	8	7	6	5	4	3	2	1
HEIGHTS												
Ḃ TO FAIRBODY	2-0-0	1-9-5	1-7-6	1-5-6	1-4-0	1-2-6	1-2-1	1-2-1	1-2-4	1-3-2	1-4-2	1-5-6
" B I	2-3-4	2-1-0	1-10-2	1-8-0	1-6-4	1-4-6	1-5-1	1-5-6	1-7-0	1-9-5	2-3-4	—
" " BOOTTOP	2-3-0	2-2-3	2-2-0	2-1-6	2-1-6	2-1-6	2-1-7	2-2-1	2-2-4	2-2-7	2-3-3	2-3-7
" " SHEER	3-1-7	3-1-1	3-0-4	3-0-1	3-0-2	3-0-4	3-0-6	3-1-3	3-2-3	3-3-4	3-4-7	3-6-2
HALF-BREADTHS												
Ḃ TO 18' WL	—	0-0-0	0-1-2	0-0-6	0-10-6	1-3-3	1-3-3	1-1-0	0-10-1	0-6-4	0-3-1	0-0-5
" " 24" WL	0-0-0	0-9-4	1-5-5	1-10-3	2-0-5	2-1-4	2-0-4	1-10-0	1-6-6	1-2-2	0-9-5	0-4-7
" " BOOTTOP	1-4-3	1-8-7	2-0-1	2-1-6	2-1-6	2-2-5	2-1-7	1-11-5	1-8-4	1-4-3	0-11-7	0-6-3
" " 30" WL	1-5-6	1-9-4	2-0-5	2-2-7	2-4-1	2-4-3	2-3-4	2-1-5	1-10-3	1-6-1	1-1-2	0-7-0
" " SHEER	1-11-2	2-3-7	2-3-7	2-5-1	2-5-5	2-5-7	2-5-3	2-4-0	2-1-4	1-9-6	1-4-5	0-9-6

Ⓑ KEEL SECTION:

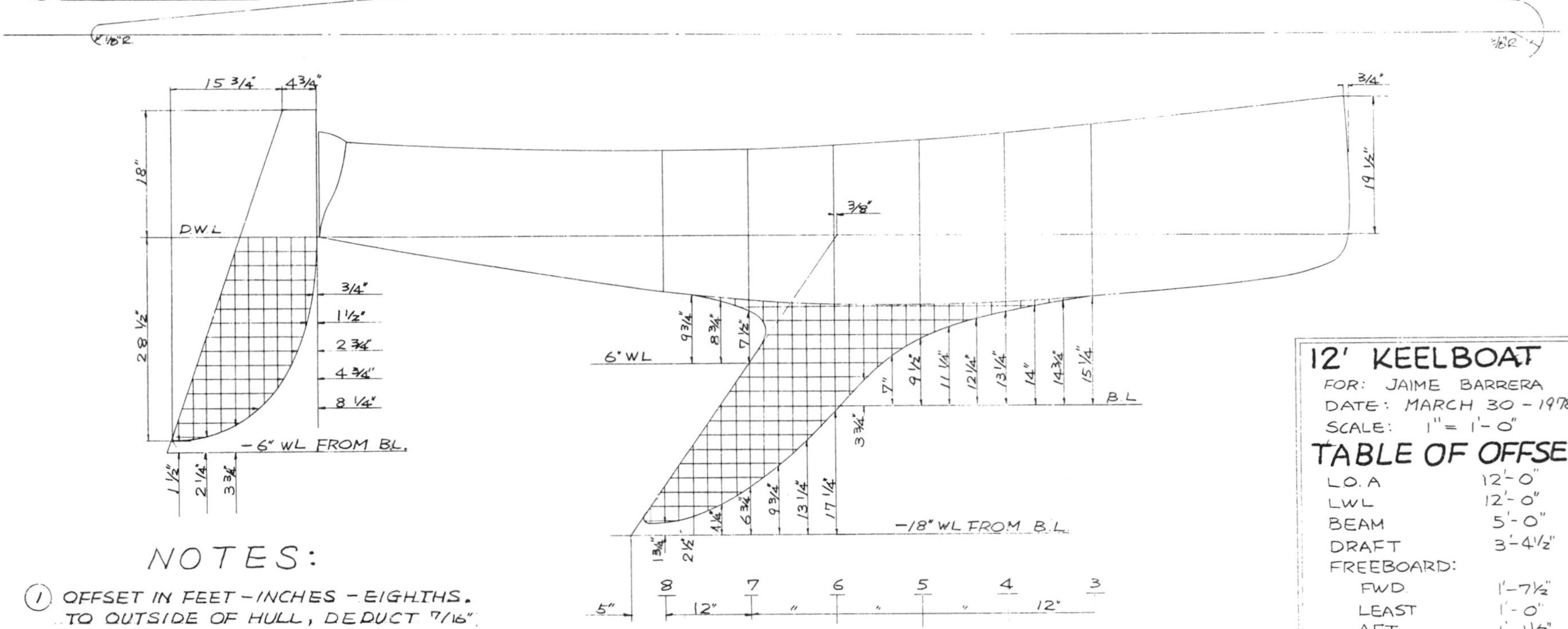

NOTES:

(1) OFFSET IN FEET - INCHES - EIGHTHS.
TO OUTSIDE OF HULL, DEDUCT 7/16"
FOR SHAPE OF OUT SIDE OF MOLD
FRAMES.

(2) OFFSETS AT STATION 12 FOR FAIRING
PURPOSES ONLY.

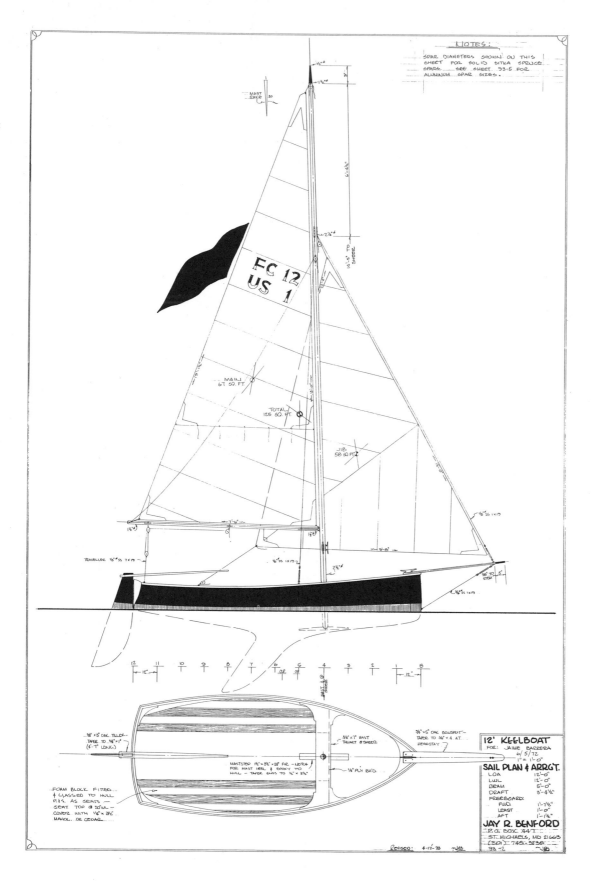

NOTES:

SPAR DIAMETERS SHOWN ON THIS
SHEET FOR SOLID SITKA SPRUCE
SPARS. SEE SHEET 93-5 FOR
ALUMINUM SPAR SIZES.

12' KEELBOAT
FOR: JAIME BARRERA
6/5/72
1" = 1'-0"

SAIL PLAN & ARR'G'T.

LOA	12'-0"
LWL	12'-0"
BEAM	5'-0"
DRAFT	3'-4½"
FREEBOARD:	
FW'D.	1'-7½"
LEAST	1'-0"
AFT	1'-1⅛"

JAY R. BENFORD
P.O. BOX 447
ST. MICHAELS, MD 21663
(301) 745-3838
93-2

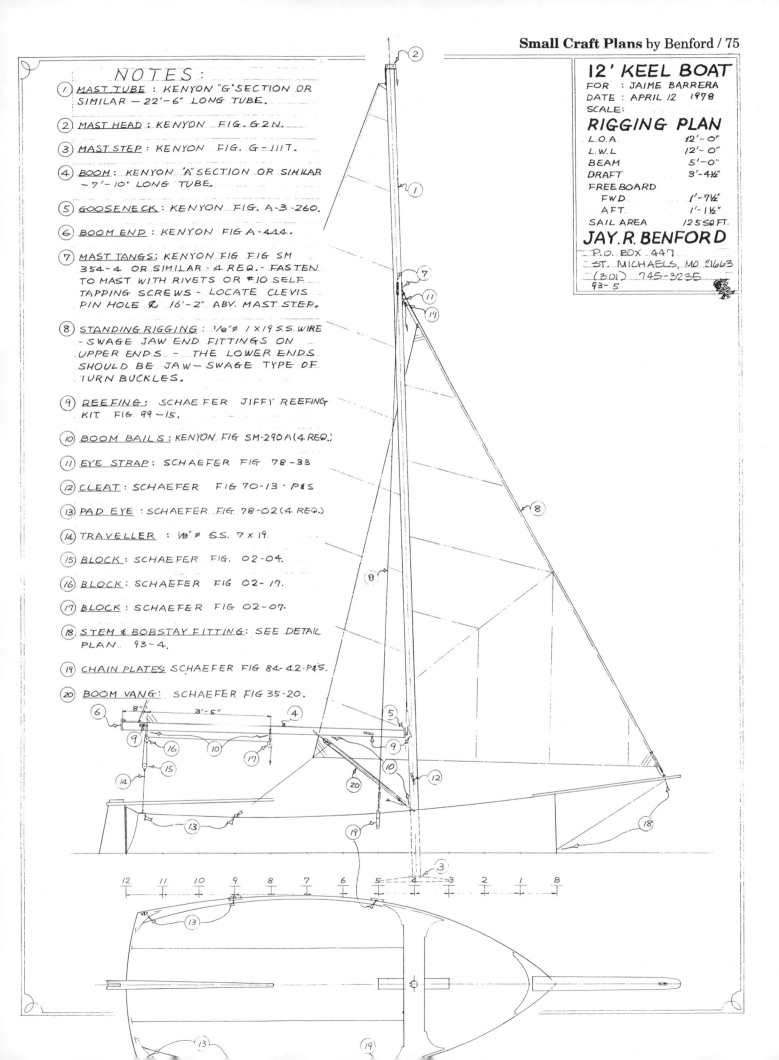

NOTES :

(1) MAST TUBE : KENYON "G" SECTION OR SIMILAR — 22'-6" LONG TUBE.

(2) MAST HEAD : KENYON FIG. G2N.

(3) MAST STEP : KENYON FIG. G-111T.

(4) BOOM : KENYON 'A" SECTION OR SIMILAR — 7'-10" LONG TUBE.

(5) GOOSENECK : KENYON FIG. A-3-260.

(6) BOOM END : KENYON FIG A-444.

(7) MAST TANGS : KENYON FIG. FIG SM 354-4 OR SIMILAR - 4 REQ. - FASTEN TO MAST WITH RIVETS OR #10 SELF TAPPING SCREWS - LOCATE CLEVIS PIN HOLE @ 16'-2" ABV. MAST STEP.

(8) STANDING RIGGING : 1/8"∅ 1 X 19 S.S. WIRE - SWAGE JAW END FITTINGS ON UPPER ENDS - THE LOWER ENDS SHOULD BE JAW — SWAGE TYPE OF TURN BUCKLES.

(9) REEFING : SCHAEFER JIFFY REEFING KIT FIG 99-15.

(10) BOOM BAILS : KENYON FIG SM-290A (4 REQ.)

(11) EYE STRAP : SCHAEFER FIG 78-33

(12) CLEAT : SCHAEFER FIG 70-13 - P&S

(13) PAD EYE : SCHAEFER FIG 78-02 (4 REQ.)

(14) TRAVELLER : 1/8"∅ S.S. 7 X 19.

(15) BLOCK : SCHAEFER FIG. 02-04.

(16) BLOCK : SCHAEFER FIG 02-17.

(17) BLOCK : SCHAEFER FIG 02-07.

(18) STEM & BOBSTAY FITTING : SEE DETAIL PLAN. 93-4.

(19) CHAIN PLATES : SCHAEFER FIG 84-42 · P&S.

(20) BOOM VANG : SCHAEFER FIG 35-20.

12' KEEL BOAT
FOR : JAIME BARRERA
DATE : APRIL 12 1978
SCALE:

RIGGING PLAN

L.O.A.	12'-0"
L.W.L	12'-0"
BEAM	5'-0"
DRAFT	3'-4½"
FREEBOARD	
FWD.	1'-7½"
AFT.	1'-1½"
SAIL AREA	125 SQ.FT.

JAY. R. BENFORD
P.O. BOX 447
ST. MICHAELS, MD 21663
(301) 745-3235
93-5

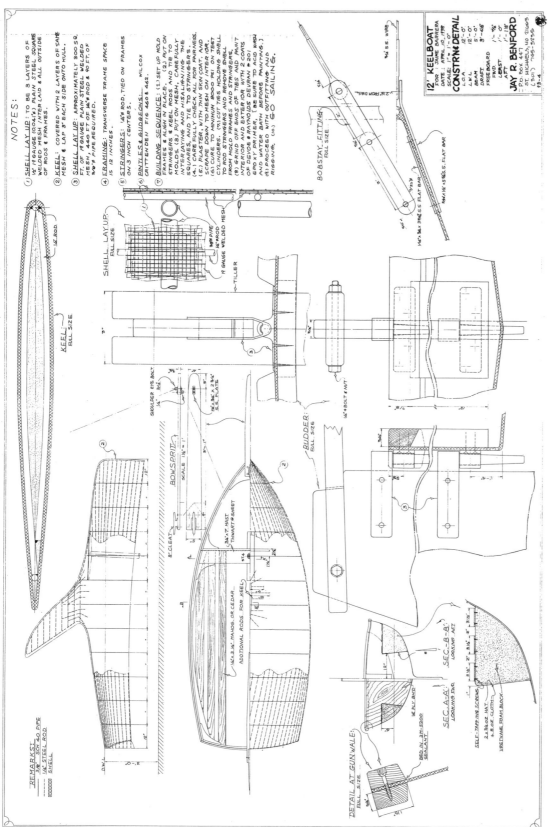

Chapter 13
16′ Sailing Tender

CONCH AD LIBITUM was commissioned by a family man who cruised with several active kids on a Grand Banks 36. He wanted a boat the kids could use for beachcombing that would be safe for them to use. The kids should be able to experience more about rowing and sailing in the new boat. The final requirement was that the new boat must be towed behind the GB36 at 9 knots between anchorages.

Paul Schweiss did an excellent job of building her and Dick Wagner did the first trials at his Old Boathouse in Seattle. I had a chance to sail her shortly afterwards and agreed with Dick's conclusion that the long keel was not very good for tacking. We decided to add a daggerboard as the way to give her something to pivot on.

This proved successful and she tacked well on it. In towing trials we decided she would need a cap for the daggerboard trunk too, to stop the water spurting in there. This was held in place by the same shock cords that held the daggerboard.

This sort of daggerboard trunk closure is well to fit on any boat that is to be towed or operated under outboard motor power. It reduces bailing later on and keeps the towing load on the painter light.

The color photo on the back cover of this book shows CONCH AD LIBITUM being rowed with both pairs of oars in use, plus the rudder and tiller in place for steering control. Also readily seen are the three mast holes for the two masts. These permit using both sails in light airs and one of the two sails, in the middle position, in heavier going.

We gave her substantial scantlings to survive repeated beachings and other adventures. I reckoned her all up weight came to a bit over 300 pounds, making her fell quite sturdy. In fact, two of us could stand on her side decks and still have a couple inches of freeboard left. This made her quite safe for the lively young crewmembers climbing in and out of her, and when they were moving around her.

The spars stowed inside her, being designed shorter than the boat. We had a fitted cover made, and kept it in place, with the rudder, board, and rig all stowed inside for towing on a cruise.

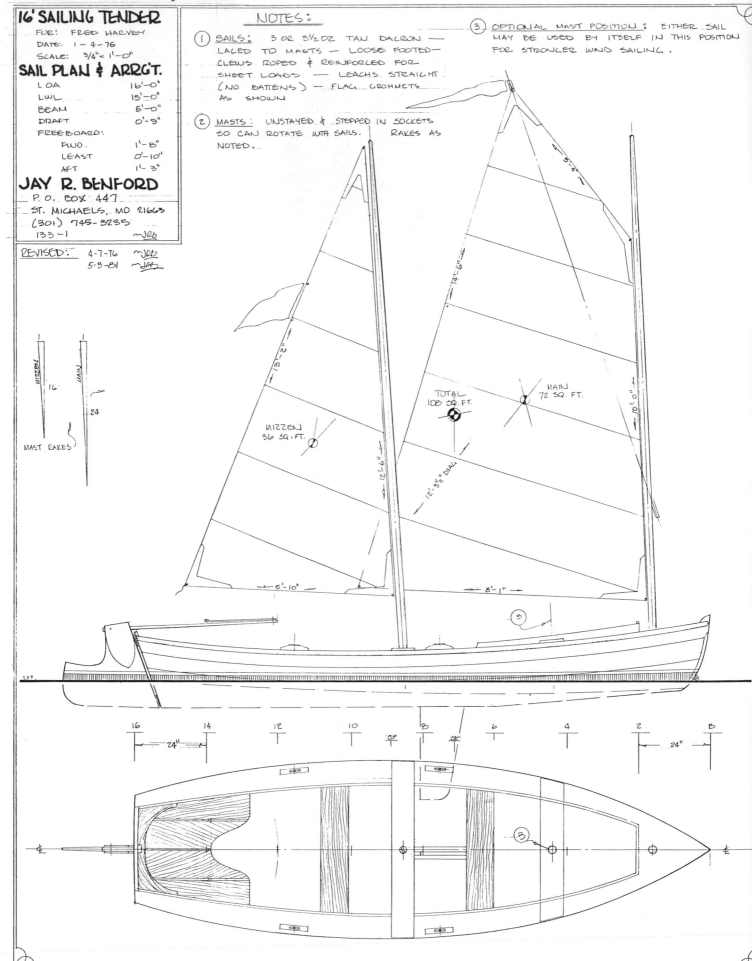

16' SAILING TENDER

FOR: FRED HARVEY
DATE: 1-4-76
SCALE: 3/4" = 1'-0"

SAIL PLAN & ARRG'T.

LOA	16'-0"
LWL	15'-0"
BEAM	5'-0"
DRAFT	0'-9"
FREEBOARD:	
FWD.	1'-8"
LEAST	0'-10"
AFT	1'-3"

JAY R. BENFORD

P. O. BOX 447
ST. MICHAELS, MD 21663
(301) 745-3235
133-1   JRB

REVISED: 4-7-76   JRB
            5-3-81   JRB

NOTES:

① SAILS: 3 OR 3½ OZ TAN DACRON — LACED TO MASTS — LOOSE FOOTED — CLEWS ROPED & REINFORCED FOR SHEET LOADS — LEACHS STRAIGHT (NO BATTENS) — FLAG GROMMETS AS SHOWN

② MASTS: UNSTAYED & STEPPED IN SOCKETS SO CAN ROTATE WITH SAILS. RAKES AS NOTED.

③ OPTIONAL MAST POSITION: EITHER SAIL MAY BE USED BY ITSELF IN THIS POSITION FOR STRONGER WIND SAILING.

MAST RAKES

MIZZEN   16
MAIN   24

MIZZEN 36 SQ. FT.

TOTAL 108 SQ. FT.

MAIN 72 SQ. FT.

NOTES:

1. LINES & OFFSETS IN FEET-INCHES-EIGHTHS TO OUTSIDE OF PLANKING. DEDUCT FOR PLANKING AS DIRECTED. LINES MUST BE LOFTED FULL SIZE — DO NOT SCALE PRINTS!

2. OFFSETS AT STA. 16 FOR FAIRING PURPOSES — ANGLE & SHAPE TRANSOM AS SHOWN.

3. THESE PLANS ARE THE PROPERTY OF THE DESIGNERS & MAY BE USED ONLY AS AUTHORIZED BY THE DESIGNERS IN WRITING.

4. NO MORE THAN ONE BOAT MAY BE BUILT FROM THESE PLANS WITHOUT PRIOR WRITTEN PERMISSION FROM THE DESIGNERS.

5. ANY ALTERATION FROM THESE PLANS RELIEVES THE DESIGNERS FROM ANY FURTHER RESPONSIBILITY.

6. BOOTTOP OFFSETS TO TOP EDGE OF 1" HIGH STRIPE.

7. CUTWATER 1" (1½" HALF-SIDING)

8. KEEL 1½" (¾" HALF-SIDING) RADIUS CORNERS AS DIRECTED

Title Block

16' SAILING TENDER

FOR: FRED HARVEY
DATE: 3-16-76
SCALE: ¾" = 1'-0"

LINES & OFFSETS

LOA	16'-0"
LWL	15'-0"
BEAM	5'-0"
DRAFT	0'-5"

FREEBOARD:
FWD. 1'-8"
LEAST 0'-10"
AFT 1'-5"

JAY R. BENFORD

P.O. BOX 447
ST. MICHAELS, MD 21663
(301) 745-3255

133-2

Offsets Table

STATION	16	14	12	10	8	6	4	2
HEIGHTS								
℄ TO KEEL	0-3-0	0-3-1	0-3-2	0-3-3	0-3-4	0-3-5	0-5-5	0-7-5
℄ TO BOTTOM	1-0-4	0-10-6	0-9-5	0-8-5	0-7-7	0-7-6	0-8-2	0-9-0
℄ TO BOOTTOP	1-3-5	1-3-1	1-5-0	1-3-0	1-2-1	1-3-1	1-3-4	1-5-6
℄ TO SHEER	2-3-0	1-11-7	1-10-3	1-10-0	2-0-1	1-11-3	2-1-3	2-4-2
HALF-BREADTHS								
℄ TO CHINE	0-10-7	1-5-3	1-9-6	1-11-6	1-11-5	1-8-2	1-1-1	0-5-7
℄ TO SHEER	1-9-2	2-0-5	2-4-2	2-5-7	2-5-6	2-3-3	1-10-5	1-1-4

PLANK LAYOUT:
NO SCALE

PARALLEL LINES SPACED 1-PLANK THICKNESS APART — LAY OUT AS SHOWN

LOFTED SHEER

LOFTED CHINE

2"x2" SQUARES

TAPER KEEL TO 1⅛" FROM 14 TO TRAILING EDGE

LWL

SHEER
CHINE
KEEL

24'

16

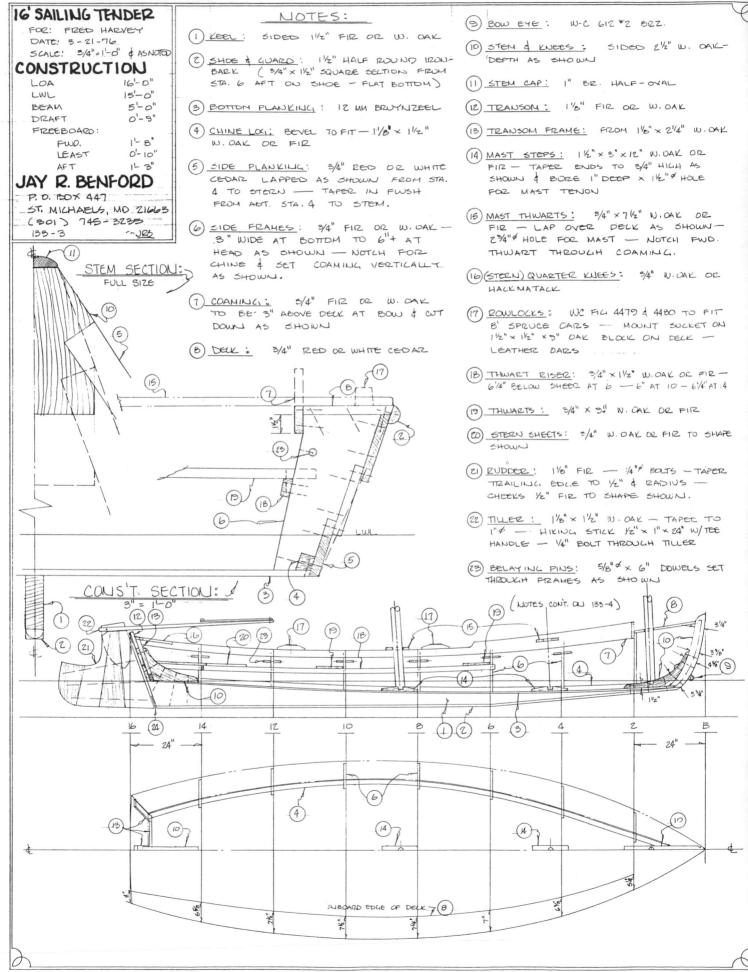

16' SAILING TENDER
FOR: FRED HARVEY
DATE: 3-21-76
SCALE: 3/4"=1'-0" & AS NOTED

CONSTRUCTION

LOA	16'-0"
LWL	15'-0"
BEAM	5'-0"
DRAFT	0'-9"
FREEBOARD:	
FWD.	1'-8"
LEAST	0'-10"
AFT	1'-3"

JAY R. BENFORD
P.O. BOX 447
ST. MICHAELS, MD. 21663
(301) 745-3235
133-3   ~JRB

NOTES:

① KEEL: SIDED 1½" FIR OR W. OAK

② SHOE & GUARD: 1½" HALF ROUND IRON-BARK (3/4" x 1½" SQUARE SECTION FROM STA. 6 AFT ON SHOE — FLAT BOTTOM)

③ BOTTOM PLANKING: 12 MM BRUYNZEEL

④ CHINE LOG: BEVEL TO FIT — 1⅛" x 1½" W. OAK OR FIR

⑤ SIDE PLANKING: 3/4" RED OR WHITE CEDAR LAPPED AS SHOWN FROM STA. 4 TO STERN — TAPER IN FLUSH FROM ABT. STA. 4 TO STEM.

⑥ SIDE FRAMES: 3/4" FIR OR W. OAK — 3" WIDE AT BOTTOM TO 6"+ AT HEAD AS SHOWN — NOTCH FOR CHINE & SET COAMING VERTICALLY AS SHOWN.

⑦ COAMING: 5/4" FIR OR W. OAK TO BE 3" ABOVE DECK AT BOW & CUT DOWN AS SHOWN

⑧ DECK: 3/4" RED OR WHITE CEDAR

⑨ BOW EYE: W-C 612 #2 BRZ.

⑩ STEM & KNEES: SIDED 2½" W. OAK — DEPTH AS SHOWN

⑪ STEM CAP: 1" BR. HALF-OVAL

⑫ TRANSOM: 1⅛" FIR OR W. OAK

⑬ TRANSOM FRAME: FROM 1⅛" x 2¼" W. OAK

⑭ MAST STEPS: 1½" x 3" x 12" W. OAK OR FIR — TAPER ENDS TO 3/4" HIGH AS SHOWN & BORE 1" DEEP x 1½"∅ HOLE FOR MAST TENON

⑮ MAST THWARTS: 3/4" x 7½" W. OAK OR FIR — LAP OVER DECK AS SHOWN — 2¾"∅ HOLE FOR MAST — NOTCH FWD. THWART THROUGH COAMING.

⑯ (STERN) QUARTER KNEES: 3/4" W. OAK OR HACKMATACK

⑰ ROWLOCKS: WC FIG 4479 & 4480 TO FIT 8' SPRUCE OARS — MOUNT SOCKET ON 1½" x 1½" x 9" OAK BLOCK ON DECK — LEATHER OARS

⑱ THWART RISER: 3/4" x 1½" W. OAK OR FIR — 6¼" BELOW SHEER AT 6 — 6" AT 10 — 6¼" AT 4

⑲ THWARTS: 3/4" x 9½" W. OAK OR FIR

⑳ STERN SHEETS: 3/4" W. OAK OR FIR TO SHAPE SHOWN

㉑ RUDDER: 1⅛" FIR — 1/4"∅ BOLTS — TAPER TRAILING EDGE TO ½" & RADIUS — CHEEKS ½" FIR TO SHAPE SHOWN.

㉒ TILLER: 1⅛" x 1½" W. OAK — TAPER TO 1"∅ — HIKING STICK ½" x 1" x 24" W/ TEE HANDLE — 1/4" BOLT THROUGH TILLER

㉓ BELAYING PINS: 5/8"∅ x 6" DOWELS SET THROUGH FRAMES AS SHOWN

STEM SECTION:
FULL SIZE

CONS'T. SECTION:
3" = 1'-0"

(NOTES CONT. ON 133-4)

INBOARD EDGE OF DECK

16' SAILING TENDER

FOR: FRED HARVEY
DATE: 4-7-76
SCALE: 3/4"= 1'-0" & AS NOTED

SPARS & DETAILS

LOA	16'-0"
LWL	15'-0"
BEAM	5'-0"
DRAFT	0'-9"
FREEBOARD:	
FWD.	1'-8"
LEAST	0'-10"
AFT	1'-3"

JAY R. BENFORD

P.O. BOX 447
ST. MICHAELS, MD 21663
(301) 745-3235
133-4

NOTES:

✳ THESE NOTES CONTINUED FROM SHEET 133-3

(24) PINTLES & GUDGEONS: W-C FIG. 460 & 462 (& 4601 GUDGEON STRAP) - BRZ.

(25) MASTS: SITKA SPRUCE TO SIZE SHOWN (NOTE — 1 3/8" RADIUS IS 2 3/4" DIAMETER) - PROVIDE HOLES FOR TACK, THROAT & HEAD AS DIRECTED — BOTH MASTS SAME SIZE

(26) SPRIT: SITKA SPRUCE TO SIZE SHOWN

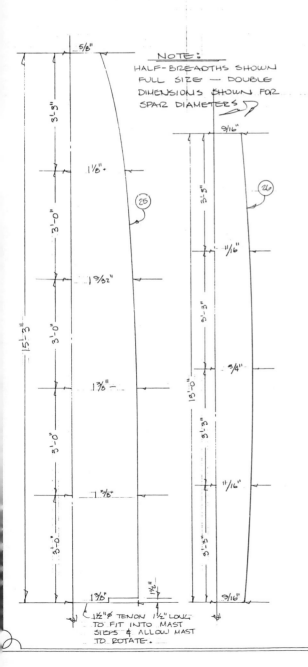

NOTE:
HALF-BREADTHS SHOWN
FULL SIZE — DOUBLE
DIMENSIONS SHOWN FOR
SPAR DIAMETERS

1 1/2"Ø TENON 1 1/2" LONG
TO FIT INTO MAST
STEPS & ALLOW MAST
TO ROTATE.

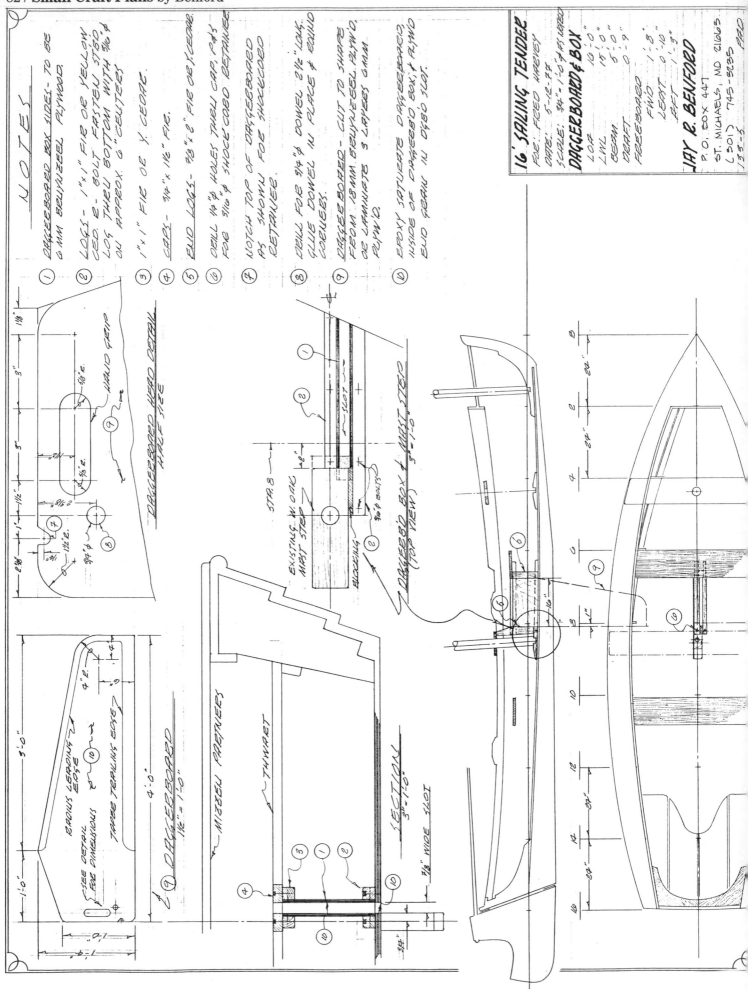

NOTES

1. DAGGERBOARD BOX SIDES - TO BE 6 MM BRUYNZEEL PLYWOOD.

2. LOGS - 1" x 1" FIR OR YELLOW CED & E-BOLT FASTEN STEP TO LOG THRU BOTTOM WITH 5/16 ∅ ON APPROX. 6" CENTERS.

3. CAPS - 3/4" x 1 1/2" FIR.

4. 1" x 1" FIR OR Y. CEDAR.

5. END LOGS - 7/8" x 2" FIR OR Y. CEDAR.

6. DRILL 1 1/8" ∅ HOLES THRU CAP #3 FOR 5/16" ∅ SHOCK CORD RETAINER.

7. NOTCH TOP OF DAGGERBOARD AS SHOWN FOR SHOCKCORD RETAINER.

8. DRILL FOR 3/4" ∅ DOWEL 2 1/2" LONG. GLUE DOWEL IN PLACE & ROUND CORNERS.

9. DAGGERBOARD - CUT TO SHAPE FROM 18 MM BRUYNZEEL PLYW'D. OR LAMINATE 3 LAYERS 6MM PLYW'D.

10. EPOXY SATURATE DAGGERBOARD, INSIDE OF DAGGERBD BOX & PLYWD END GRAIN IN DAGGBD SLOT.

16' SAILING TENDER

FOR: FRED HARDISTY
DATE: 5-12-79
SCALE: 3/4" = 1'-0" AS NOTED

DAGGERBOARD & BOX

JAY R. BENFORD
P.O. BOX 447
ST. MICHAELS, MD 21663
(301) 745-3235
135-3

LOA	16'-0"	
LWL	15'-0"	
BEAM	5'-6"	
DRAFT	0'-9"	
FREEBOARD		
FWD	1'-8"	
LEAST	0'-10"	
AFT	1'-3"	

DAGGERBOARD HEAD DETAIL HALF SIZE

HAND GRIP

DAGGERBOARD
1 1/2" = 1'-0"

RADIUS LEADING EDGE

SEE DETAIL FOR DIMENSIONS

TAPER TRAILING EDGE

MIZZEN PARTNERS

THWART

EXISTING W. OAK MAST STEP

STA. 8

DAGGERBD BOX & MAST STEP
(TOP VIEW)
3" = 1'-0"

SLOT

BLOCKING

5/16" ∅ BOLTS

SECTION
3" = 1'-0"

7/8" WIDE SLOT

3/4"

Chapter 14
18' Cat Ketch

This design followed the 16' Sailing Tender by several years. During this interval, I'd had quite a bit of experience with the 16-footer as we looked after her for ten to eleven months a year.

This experience with CONCH AD LIBITUM led to a number of thoughts and ideas on how she could be changed and/or improved.

The commission for the 18' Cat Ketch came from a client wanting to try out sailing a cat ketch on a smaller scale before owning a larger cruising boat with the same rig. He felt that this would give him useful experience and knowledge about how to sail a cat ketch and confirm his desire to own a larger one.

In creating her, we knew that she was to be sailed off a trailer. Reducing her structural weights would make this much easier to do, and make her more lively to sail.

We also decided to increase her sail area, based on our experience with the 16-footer. We came to realize that most all the sailing of a small pleasure craft was in lighter wind conditions, rather than thrashing through heavy weather. More sail area would make her more fun to sail, and we've done that with the 18-footer.

We've also given her a longer foredeck. This will provide shelter for bagged camping gear and a place for kids to hide from the weather. We've kept the cockpits more open, making more room for camping aboard.

There is only one rowing position. This is aft where she could be rowed by the helmsman. Another position could be added forward, but this would mean adding another thwart, taking away from the open layout.

For a heavier duty version of this boat, I would suggest adding 1/8" to the plywood thickness of the hull and deck. This will add about 150 to 200 pounds to her structure. A heavier boat will carry her way better through some conditions, but I would not recommend doing this unless your service needs a very rugged boat.

NOTES:

1. LINES & OFFSETS IN FEET-INCHES-EIGHTHS TO OUTSIDE OF PLANKING. DEDUCT FOR MOLD FRAMES AS REQUIRED.
2. LINES MUST BE LOFTED & FAIRED FULL SIZE. DO NOT SCALE PRINTS.
3. BOOTOP OFFSETS TO TOP EDGE OF BOOT STRIPE — STRIPE IS 1" HIGH IN PROFILE FULL LENGTH.
4. THESE PLANS ARE THE PROPERTY OF THE DESIGNER & MAY BE USED ONLY AS AUTHORIZED BY THE DESIGNER IN WRITING.
5. ANY ALTERATION FROM THESE PLANS RELIEVES THE DESIGNER FROM ANY FURTHER RESPONSIBILITY.
6. IT IS UNDERSTOOD THAT NO MORE THAN ONE BOAT WILL BE BUILT FROM THESE PLANS WITHOUT WRITTEN PERMISSION FROM THE DESIGNER.

⑦ HALF-SIDING OF STEM IS 0-0-3.
⑧ OFFSETS IN BRACKETS (0-0-0) FOR FAIRING PURPOSES.

STATION	18	16	14	12	10	8	6	4	2
HEIGHTS									
₵ TO CHINE	(1-0-7)	0-11-1	0-9-5	0-8-4	0-8-0	0-8-2	0-8-5	0-7-4	0-11-0
" BOOTOP ③									
" SHEER	3-0-0	2-8-3	2-6-0	2-6-1	2-6-5	2-7-6	2-9-3	2-11-0	3-2-6
HALF-BREADTHS									
₵ TO CHINE	(1-3-4)	1-7-1	1-9-7	1-11-4	2-0-0	1-10-3	1-6-5	1-0-6	0-5-0
" SHEER	2-2-0	2-2-6	2-9-2	2-11-2	3-0-0	2-10-6	2-7-2	2-1-3	1-3-3

DECK CAMBER: 2
3"=1'-0"

DAGGERBOARD!
1½"=1'-0"

RADIUSED EDGE
TAPER
NOTCH FOR MENDING CORD
¾"Ø PIN 3" LONG
1¼"×4" SLOT

SHEER
CHINE
SKEG
CURVE OF AREA'S = 1½" 1FT²

JAY R. BENFORD ☆ 18' CAT KETCH ☆ LINES & OFFSETS
BOX 447 ST. MICHAELS, MD 21663 FOR: AL DEFALCO   4/13/82 ~ 3/4"=1'-0" ~ JRB

DESIGN Nº 204
SHEET Nº 1

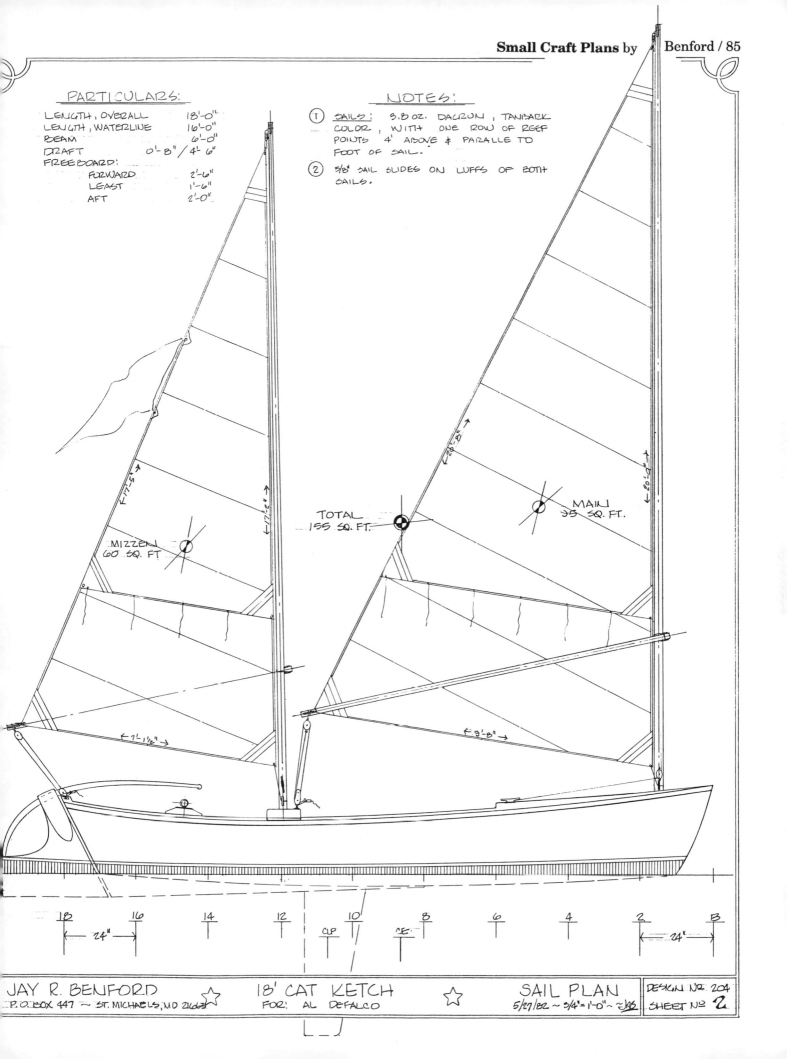

PARTICULARS:

LENGTH, OVERALL   18'-0"
LENGTH, WATERLINE   16'-0"
BEAM   6'-0"
DRAFT   0'-8" / 4'-6"
FREEBOARD:
    FORWARD   2'-6"
    LEAST   1'-6"
    AFT   2'-0"

NOTES:

① SAILS: 3.8 OZ. DACRON, TANBARK COLOR, WITH ONE ROW OF REEF POINTS 4' ABOVE & PARALLE TO FOOT OF SAIL.

② 5/8" SAIL SLIDES ON LUFFS OF BOTH SAILS.

MIZZEN
60 SQ. FT.

TOTAL
155 SQ. FT.

MAIN
95 SQ. FT.

JAY R. BENFORD
P.O. BOX 447 ~ ST. MICHAELS, MD 21663

18' CAT KETCH
FOR: AL DEFALCO

SAIL PLAN
5/27/82 ~ 3/4"=1'-0" ~

DESIGN Nº 204
SHEET Nº 2

NOTES:

1. BOTTOM PLANKING: ½" (12MM) PLYWOOD SCARFED TO LENGTH.

2. SIDE PLANKING: ⅜" (10 MM) PLYWOOD SCARFED TO LENGTH

3. CHINE & CLAMP: FROM 1½" × 1¾" D. FIR OR Y. CEDAR — BEVEL AS REQ'D.

4. SHEER GUARD: 1½" W. OAK OR GUM HALF-ROUND

5. DECK: ⅜" PLY SCARFED TO LENGTH — 3" CAMBER IN 6'-0" BEAM.

6. CARLIN: ¾" × 1½" D. FIR OR Y. CEDAR.

7. MOLDING: FROM ½" × 1½" D. FIR OR Y. CEDAR.

8. SKEG: FROM 1½" D. FIR.

9. WORM SHOE: ½" × 1½" IRONBARK OR GUM — RUN FROM STEM TO HEEL OF SKEG.

10. STEM & KNEE: SIDED 2½" D. FIR. OR W. OAK. — NOTE NOTCH ON KNEE FOR MAST STEP.

11. STEM CAP: 1½" GUM OR IRONBARK WITH ¾" BRONZE ½-OVAL OVER — RUN ½-OVAL 12" AFT ALONG BOTTOM, WITH TIGHT BEND AT BASE OF STEM.

12. SIDE DECKS: 9" WIDTH FROM STA. 6 TO STERN.

13. TRANSOM: ¾" PLY WITH 1½" × 1¾" FRAME ALL AROUND — ½" × 3" CAP ACROSS TOP

14. LONG'L DECK FRAME: ¾" × 1½" HIGH — 7½" OFF ₵ P/S. — LET INTO 15+ SCREW TO CLAMP.

15. FO'C'SLE FRAME: 1½" × 3" ALL AROUND OPENING; ⅜" PLY BRACKETS AT CORNERS AT STATION 6.

16. DOUBLER: ⅜" PLY FITTED TO CLAMP & (14).

17. SHEATHING: DYNEL OR GLASS CLOTH SET IN EPOXY RESIN, DOUBLED OVER CHINES.

18. THWART: ¾" × 11", WITH ¾" × 1½" × 24" RISER & 1½" Ø POST SUPPORT ON ₵

19. MAST THWART: ¾" × 11" W. OAK SPRUNG TO DECK CAMBER & LAPPING ONTO SIDE-DECKS — CENTERED ON MIZZEN MAST ₵.

20. STERN KNEE: SIDED 1½"

21. MAST STEP: FROM 1½" × 5" × 12" — TAPER ENDS TO ½" × 3" — DRILL FOR MAST TENON.

22. DAGGERBOARD TRUNK: ⅜" PLY SIDES — 1½" × 1½" BOTTOM FRAMES — ⅞" × 1½" END (VERTICAL) FRAMES — LOCATE TRUNK OFF ₵ TO CLEAR SKEG — TRUNK TO HAVE 2¼" CLEAR FORE & AFT IN SLOT — ¾" × 1½" FRAMES AT TOP; 12" ABOVE DWL — AFT VERTICAL FRAME EXTENDS UP & SCREWED TO MAST THWART.

23. DAGGERBOARD: ¾" PLY — LEADING EDGE RADIUSED & TRAILING 4" TAPERED TO FINE EDGE — SEE SHEET 1 FOR OUTLINE DIMS.

DECK PLAN

DECK FRAMING

STEM SECTIONS: 6"=1'-0"

CONSTRUCTION SECTION: 3"=1'-0"

SHEER ON LOFTING

TOP

BOTTOM

DWL

CHINE ON LOFTING

RAISED ROWLOCK SOCKET (P/S & 9' OARS)

JAY R. BENFORD ☆ 18' CAT KETCH ☆ CONSTRUCTION PLAN

BOX 447 — ST. MICHAELS, MD 21663   FOR: AL DEFALCO

DESIGN Nº 204   SHEET 1/2 3

5/30/92 ~ ¾"=1'-0" & AS NOTED ~ Nº 145

NOTES:

(1) **SPARS:** TO BE SOLID SITKA SPRUCE TO DIAMETERS SHOWN. CURVED FORWARD ENDS OF SPRITS MAY BE LAMINATED TO SHAPE.

(2) **SAIL TRACKS:** SCHAEFER 75-05 5/8" TRACK ON AFT SIDE OF BOTH MASTS.

(3) **HALYARD BLOCKS:** BEE BLOCK P/S. ON EACH MASTHEAD TO HOLD STROP FOR HALYARD BLOCK (SCHAEFER 303-05 BLOCKS)

(4) **TENONS:** 1¼"ø × 1" LONG TO EXTEND INTO MORTICE IN MAST STEP ON MAIN & MIZZEN MASTS.

(5) **MAIN HALYARD:** RUNS THROUGH MASTHEAD BLOCK TO CHEEK BLOCK ON MAST JUST ABOVE DECK TO CLEAT ON DECK JUST FWD. OF STA. 6.   5/16"ø DACRON.

(6) **MIZZEN HALYARD:** RUNS THROUGH MASTHEAD BLOCK TO CLEAT ON MAST JUST ABOVE THWART.   5/16"ø DACRON.

(7) **MIZZEN SHEET:** STARTS AT PADEYE 9" OFF ₵ TO PORT; GOES TO BLOCK (SCHAEFER 303-05) AT END OF SPRIT; THENCE TO (SCHAEFER 69-16) SWIVEL BLOCK WITH CAM CLEAT 9" OFF ₵ TO STBD. — PROVIDE BEE BLOCKS AT EXTREME AFT END OF SPRIT FOR STROP FOR BLOCK & EXTRA HOLES FOR OUTHAUL LINES. 5/16"ø DACRON.

(8) **MAIN SHEET:** PROVIDE BEE BLOCKS AT EXTREME AFT END OF SPRIT FOR STROP FOR BLOCK & EXTRA HOLES FOR OUTHAUL LINES. (SCHAEFER 303-15) BLOCK W/BECKET ON BOOM & (SCHAEFER 69-42) SWIVEL FIDDLE BLOCK W/CAM CLEAT ON ₵ ON MIZZEN MAST THWART.   5/16"ø DACRON.

(9) **DOWNHAULS:** 5/16"ø DACRON TAILS ON TACKS LEAD TO BEE BLOCKS AT BASE OF MASTS JUST ABOVE DECK.

(10) **OUTHAULS:** 3/16"ø DACRON TIED THROUGH EXTRA HOLES IN SHEET BLOCK BEE BLOCKS.

(11) **SNOTTERS:** 3/16"ø DACRON LOOPED AROUND MAST & TIED TO FORWARD END OF SPRIT — PROVIDE BEE BLOCK AT EXTREME FORWARD END FOR SNOTTER.

(12) **REEFING LINES:** ¼"ø DACRON — FOR TYING REEF CRINGLES DOWN TO LEVEL OF FOOT.

(13) **SPRITS:** MIZZEN 1½"ø OVER FORWARD HALF & TAPERING TO 1¼"ø AFT — MAIN 1¾"ø FOR FORWARD HALF & TAPERED TO 1½"ø AFT.

(14) **BEE BLOCKS:** FROM ½" × ½" × 2¼" HARDWOOD (DOUBLES FROM ½" × ½" × 3")

(15) **MAST RAKES:** MIZZEN RAKES AFT 1" IN 48" — MAIN SET VERTICALLY (NO RAKE).

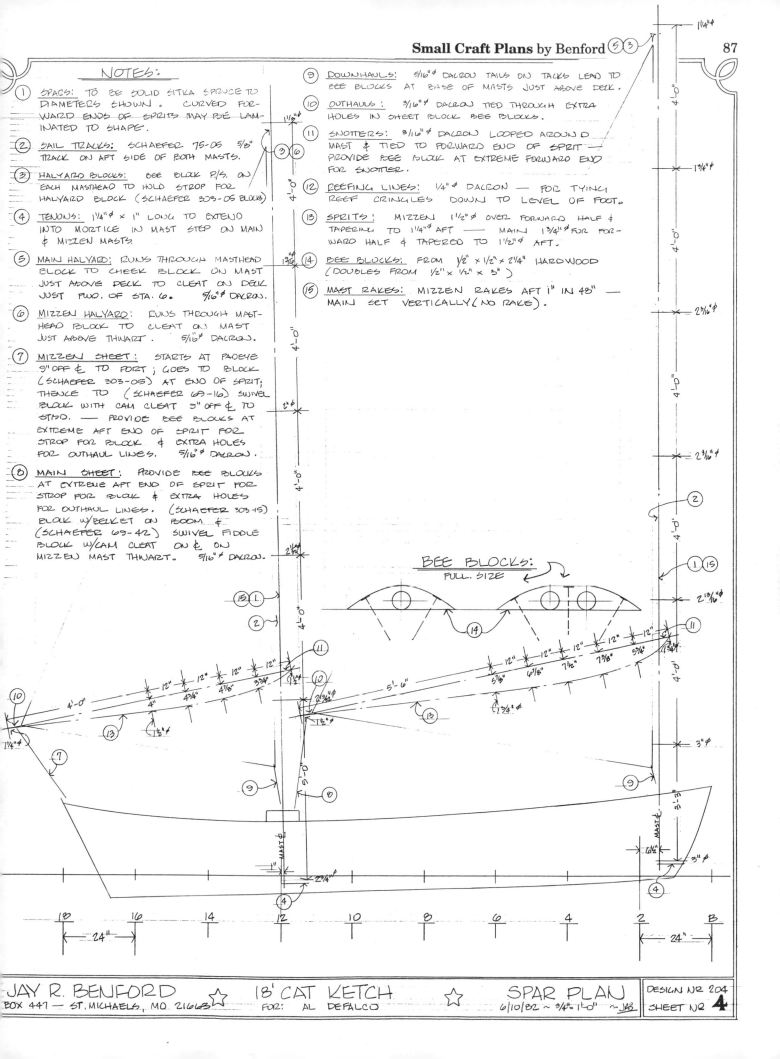

BEE BLOCKS: FULL SIZE

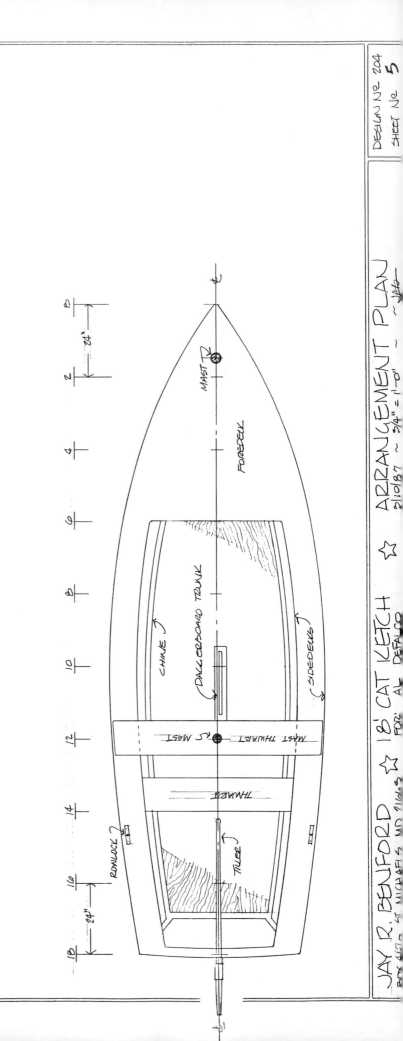

Chapter 15
18′ Texas Skiff

Modified dory skiffs, such as this one, are popular fishing and working boats in many areas of this country; in the Carolinas, on the Gulf Coast, and other areas.

She is intended for fishing and general utility work. Her open layout, with a walkway between the seats, permits easy access from bow to stern.

The design shows batten seam construction. With the battens as backing for the seams, the frames can be more widely spaced, and we've put them on the design stations on 24" centers.

Alternatively, she could be built of plywood, with perhaps 3/8" sides and 1/2" for the bottom. This would permit the elimination of the battens and the construction would probably go much more quickly.

I've shown the control station to port. This is in line with my philosophy of always putting an off center helm to port. My reasoning for this is that the danger zone is to starboard, and any passengers would also be to starboard. So, if the helmsman is looking at or talking to the person to starboard, he would be looking towards the danger zone. This is much preferred to turning your back on the danger zone and should contribute to more safe operation.

The power shown is a 70hp outboard, with suitable alternatives being in the 50 to 90hp range, depending on the speed wanted and how she will be loaded.

The fuel tank is a cylindrical tank, located where it is fully open for service access. It could also become a seat for additional passengers or when communing with the engine.

Another alternative for powering would be to build her with no notch and slot for an outboard. Then, an inboard engine with an outdrive could be fitted in this space. The additional bouyancy gained from filling in the outboard slot would offset the added weight of an outdrive engine.

A melon hood or bimini would add welcome shade and shelter. It could be integrated with a full cockpit cover with screens to turn her into a camp-cruiser.

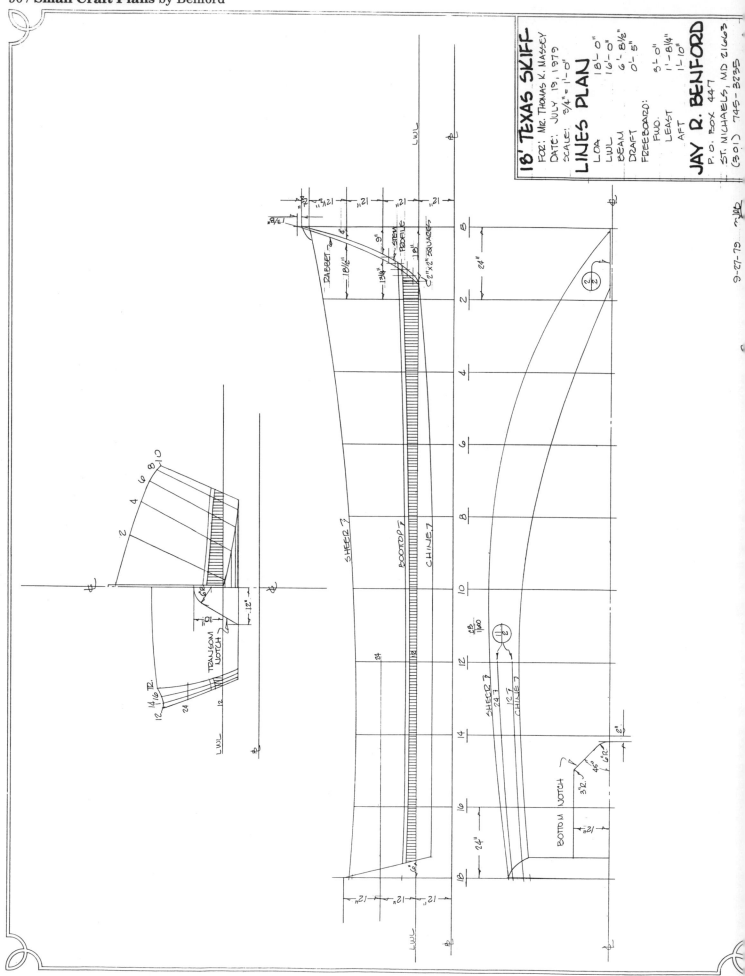

NOTES:

1. BOTTOM IS FLAT — HEIGHTS TO BOTTOM SAME AT CL AS AT CHINE.
2. HALF-SIDING OF BASSETS IS 1"
3. OFFSETS IN BRACKETS (0-0-0) FOR GUIDE IN FAIRING ONLY.
4. LINES & OFFSETS IN FEET-INCHES-EIGHTHS TO OUTSIDE OF HULL — DEDUCT FOR HULL THICKNESS AS DIRECTED.
5. LINES MUST BE LOFTED & FAIRED FULL SIZE — DO NOT SCALE PRINTS & OFFSETS.
6. ANY ALTERATION FROM THESE PLANS RELIEVES THE DESIGNERS FROM ANY FURTHER RESPONSIBILITY.
7. THESE PLANS ARE THE PROPERTY OF THE DESIGNERS & MAY BE USED ONLY AS AUTHORIZED BY THE DESIGNERS IN WRITING.
8. IT IS UNDERSTOOD THAT NO MORE THAN ONE BOAT WILL BE BUILT FROM THESE PLANS WITHOUT WRITTEN PERMISSION FROM THE DESIGNERS.
9. OFFSETS AT STATION 10 FOR FAIRING PURPOSES ONLY.
10. BOOTTOP OFFSETS TO TOP EDGE OF STRIPE. STRIPE IS 1½" HIGH IN PROFILE FULL LENGTH.
11. TOPSIDE FRAMES FORWARD OF STA. 12 ARE STRAIGHT.

18' TEXAS SKIFF

FOR: MR. THOMAS K. MASSEY
DATE: JULY 19, 1979
SCALE: AS NOTED

OFFSETS & NOTES

LOA	18'-0"
LWL	16'-0"
BEAM	6'-8½"
DRAFT	0'-5"
FREEBOARD:	
FWD.	3'-0"
LEAST	1'-8¼"
AFT	1'-10"

JAY R. BENFORD
P.O. BOX 447
ST. MICHAELS, MD 21663
(301) 745-3235
189-2

REVISED: 9-27-78
9-5-79

STATION

		18	16	14	12	10	8	6	4	2
HEIGHTS										
CL TO CHINE		(0-7-0)	0-7-0	0-7-0	0-7-0	0-7-0	0-7-2	0-7-7	0-7-2	0-11-3
LWL "	BOOTTOP	(0-4-6)	0-4-0	0-4-2	0-3-7	0-4-0	0-4-2	0-4-6+	0-5-5	0-6-5
" "	SHEER	(1-10-3)	1-8-6	1-8-2	1-8-3	1-9-2	1-10-6	2-0-7	2-3-7	2-7-6
HALF-BREADTHS										
CL TO CHINE		(2-2-2)	2-4-2	2-6-5	2-6-2	2-5-2	2-1-6	1-7-7	1-0-1	0-2-4
" "	12" WL (LWL)	(2-4-4)	2-6-2	2-7-5	2-8-3	2-8-3	2-1-6			
" "	24" WL	(2-7-7)	2-10-2	2-11-7	3-1-2					
" "	SHEER	(2-9-3)	3-0-2	3-2-3	3-3-6	3-4-2	3-2-7	2-11-2	2-4-3	1-5-1

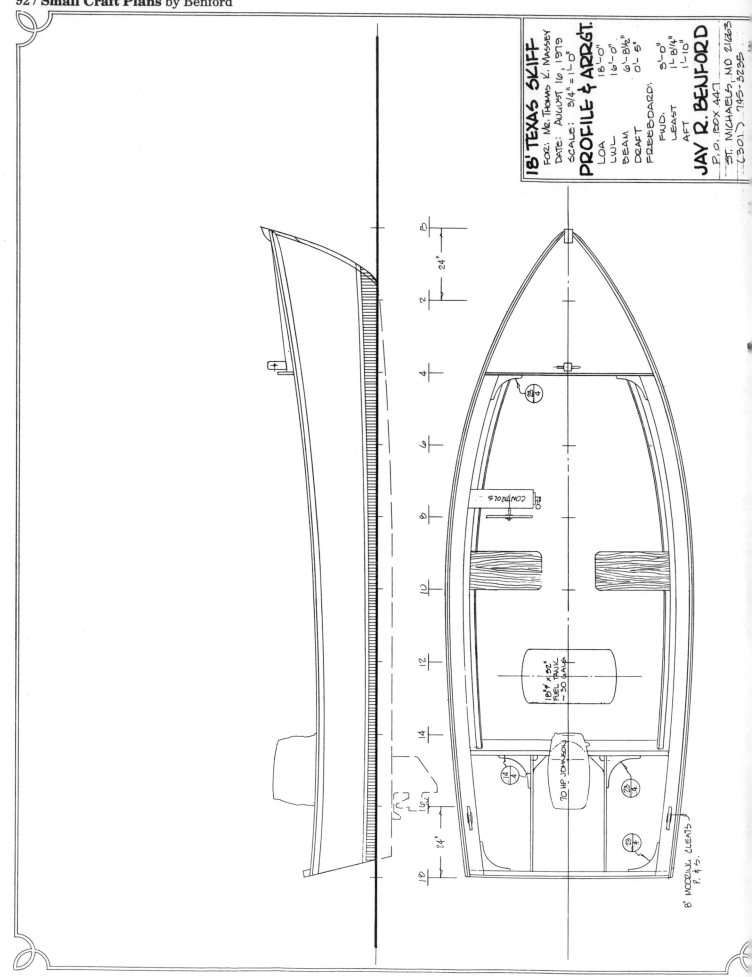

18' TEXAS SKIFF

FOR: MR. THOMAS V. MASSEY

DATE: AUGUST 16, 1979

SCALE: 3/4" = 1'-0"

PROFILE & ARRGT.

LOA	18'-0"
LWL	16'-0"
BEAM	6'-8½"
DRAFT	0'-5"
FREEBOARD:	
FWD.	3'-0"
LEAST	1'-8¾"
AFT	1'-10"

JAY R. BENFORD

P.O. BOX 447

ST. MICHAELS, MD 21663

(301) 745-3235

70 HP JOHNSON

CONTROLS

18" x 52" FUEL TANK ~ 30 GALS.

8" MOORING CLEATS P. & S.

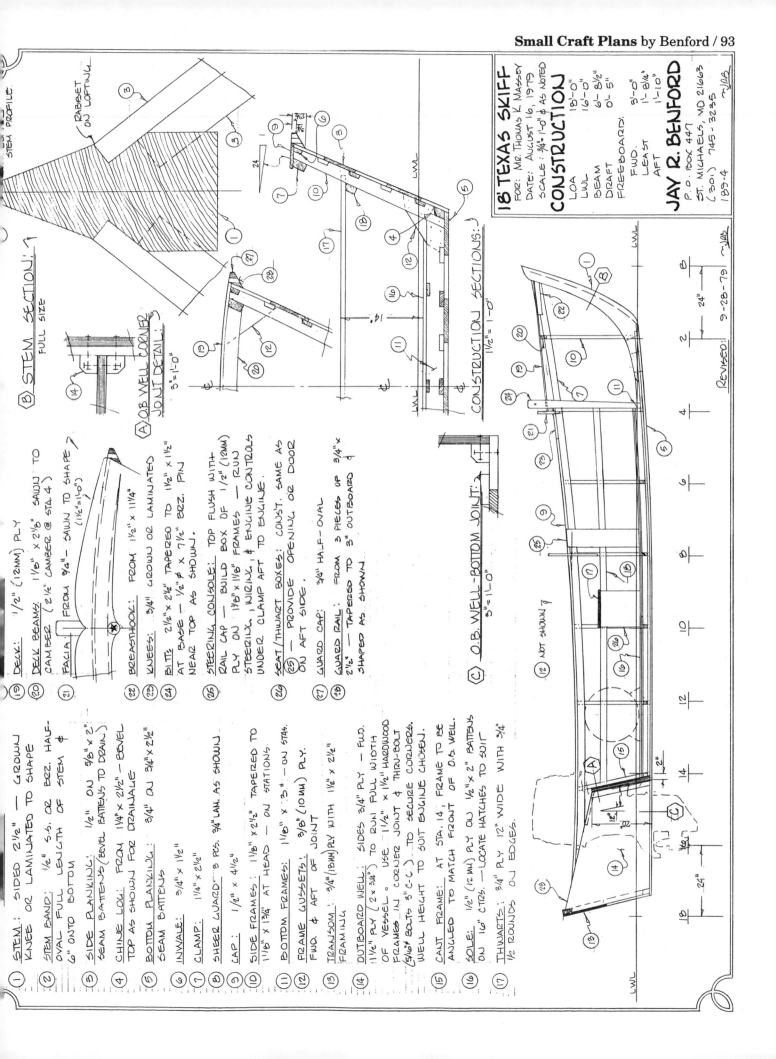

18' TEXAS SKIFF

FOR: MR. THOMAS K. MASSEY
DATE: AUGUST 16, 1979
SCALE: 3/4"=1'-0" & AS NOTED

CONSTRUCTION

LOA	18'-0"
LWL	16'-0"
BEAM	6'-8½"
DRAFT	0'-5"
FREEBOARD:	
FWD.	3'-0"
LEAST	1'-8¾"
AFT	1'-10"

JAY R. BENFORD
P.O. BOX 447
ST. MICHAELS, MD 21663
(301) 745-3235
189-4

REVISED: 9-28-79

B STEM SECTION: 1
FULL SIZE

A O.B. WELL CORNER JOINT DETAIL:
3"=1'-0"

C O.B. WELL-BOTTOM JOINT:
3"=1'-0"

CONSTRUCTION SECTIONS:
1½" = 1'-0"

STEM PROFILE:
RABBET ON LOFTING

---

① STEM: SIDED 2½" — GROWN KNEE OR LAMINATED TO SHAPE

② STEM BAND: ½" 5.5. OR BZZ. HALF-OVAL FULL LENGTH OF STEM & 6" ONTO BOTTOM

③ SIDE PLANKING: ½" ON 5/8" x 2" SEAM BATTENS (BEVEL BATTENS TO DRAIN)

④ CHINE LOG: FROM 1¼" x 2½" — BEVEL TOP AS SHOWN FOR DRAINAGE

⑤ BOTTOM PLANKING: ¾" ON ¾" x 2½" SEAM BATTENS

⑥ INWALE: ¾" x 1½"

⑦ CLAMP: 1½" x 2½"

⑧ SHEER GUARD: 3 PCS. ¾" LAM. AS SHOWN

⑨ CAP: ½" x 4½"

⑩ SIDE FRAMES: 1⅛" x 2½" TAPERED TO 1⅛" x 1¾" AT HEAD — ON STATIONS.

⑪ BOTTOM FRAMES: 1⅛" x 5" — ON STA.

⑫ FRAME GUSSETS: 3/8" (10MM) PLY. FWD. & AFT OF JOINT

⑬ TRANSOM: ¾" (18MM) PLY WITH 1½" x 2½" FRAMING

⑭ OUTBOARD WELL: SIDES ¾" PLY — FWD. 1½" PLY (2 x ¾") TO RUN FULL WIDTH OF VESSEL. USE 1½" x 1½" HARDWOOD FRAMES IN CORNER JOINT & THRU-BOLT (5/16" BOLTS 5"C-C.) TO SECURE CORNERS. WELL HEIGHT TO SUIT ENGINE CHOSEN.

⑮ CANT FRAME: AT STA.14, FRAME TO BE ANGLED TO MATCH FRONT OF O.B. WELL.

⑯ SOLE: ½" (12MM) PLY ON ½" x 2" BATTENS ON 10" CTRS. — LOCATE HATCHES TO SUIT

⑰ THWARTS: ¾" PLY 12" WIDE WITH ¾" ½ ROUNDS ON EDGES.

⑲ DECK: ½" (12MM) PLY

⑳ DECK BEAMS: 1⅛" x 2⅛" SAWN TO CAMBER (2½" CAMBER @ STA. 4)

㉑ FACIA: FROM ¾" — SAWN TO SHAPE (1½"=1'-0")

㉒ BREASTHOOK: FROM 1½" x 11¼"

㉓ KNEES: ¾" GROWN OR LAMINATED

㉔ BITS: 2½" x 2½" TAPERED TO 1½" x 1½" AT BASE — 1½" ø x 7½" BZZ. PIN NEAR TOP AS SHOWN.

㉖ STEERING CONSOLE: TOP FLUSH WITH RAIL CAP — BUILD BOX OF ½" (12MM) PLY ON 1⅛" x 1⅛" FRAMES — RUN STEERING, WIRING, & ENGINE CONTROLS UNDER CLAMP AFT TO ENGINE.

㉕ SEAT/THWART BOXES: CONST. SAME AS ㉕ — PROVIDE OPENING OR DOOR ON AFT SIDE.

㉗ GUARD CAP: ¾" HALF-OVAL

㉘ GUARD RAIL: FROM 3 PIECES OF ¾" 2½" — TAPERED TO 3" OUTBOARD & SHAPED AS SHOWN

30' SCHOONER "BELLE AMIE"
30' x 24' x 10'6" x 4'6"
Cold-molded, strip-planked,
Airex, or steel
Many alt. rigs and interiors
Study plans $11

27' CUTTER
27' x 22'6" x 8'9½" x 4'
Airex or glass
Easily converted to carvel
or cold-molded
Study plans $18.50

45½' KETCH (or CUTTER)
45'6" x 37'6" x 14' x 5'6"
Airex—easily converted to
carvel or cold-molded
Study plans $15

46' KETCH "TOKETEE"
46' x 37'6" x 13'2" x 6'
C-Flex or Airex—easily converted to carvel or cold-molded
Study plans $22

22' CRUISING CAT
22' x 20' x 9'8" x 4'6"
Airex—easily converted to
carvel or cold-molded
6'2" headroom
Study plans $11

38' KETCH
38' x 30'6" x 11' x 5'9"
Airex
Easily converted to wood
Study plans $11

More CLASSIC BOAT PLANS

These distinctive boat designs are a selection from the board of **Jay R. Benford**, shown in his *Catalog Packet* ($10 postpaid) and his book *Cruising Yachts* ($35 postpaid). To order your own copies use the coupon below or write to:

P.O. Box 447–A, St. Michaels, MD 21663

34' TOPSAIL KETCH "SUNRISE"
34'6" x 30'8" x 11'3" x 6'3"
Carvel
Alt. Great Pyramid rig
Study plans $15

20' FALSE CREEK FERRY
20' x 19' x 8' x 2'
Plywood
Many serving Expo '86
Study plans $7

32' TUG-YACHT
32' x 30' x 13' x 3'
Steel
Other sizes available
Study plans $11

37' PILOTHOUSE CUTTER "CORCOVADO"
37' x 33' x 12'4" x 5'
Cold-molded or carvel
3 rigs, 4 interiors
35' & 40' versions
Study plans $29

14' TUG "GRIVIT"
14' x 13' x 7' x 3'
Cold-molded or Airex
Tug & trawler-yacht versions
Study plans $11

19' GUNKHOLER "CATSPAW"
19'6" x 18' x 7'9" x 1'4"/4'8"
Plywood
Study plans $7

This 38' Tug Yacht is one of over 100 Distinctive Benford Designs shown in our Catalog
Packet. Send $10.00 for your own copy today.

20' SUPPLY BOAT "BATEN"
20' x 19' x 7'11½" x 2'3"
Cold-molded, carvel,
or Airex
Study plans $7

20' TUG-YACHT
20' x 18' x 8' x 2'3"
Airex (kits available)
Study plans $7

42' SOUTH SEAS TRADER
42'6" x 32' x 13'6" x 6'
Carvel, cold-molded, Airex,
or steel
5 rigs, 10 interiors
Study plans $22

32' AUXILIARY KETCH
32' x 26' x 10'7" x 4'
Strip-planked/cold-molded
Alt. cutter rig, aft cockpit
Study plans $15

23' CANOE YAWL
23' x 21' x 8'9" x 4'
Airex
Easily converted to wood
Study plans $8

17' CRUISING YAWL
17' x 15'1½" x 7' x 3'6"
Strip-planked/cold-molded
Sloop & catboat versions
Study plans $11

31' TOPSAIL KETCH
31'3" x 24'5" x 10'7" x 3'/5'9"
Cold-molded or strip-planked
Many alt. rigs & interiors
Study plans $7

30' D.E. CUTTER
30' x 27' x 9'6" x 5'
Airex—easily converted to
carvel or cold-molded
Study plans $7

Why did *Cruising Sailboat Kinetics*, "a heavily illustrated showcase of the best cruising sailboat design of the last decade," include more designs by Jay Benford than any other designer? The author, Danny Greene, is the design editor of *Cruising World* magazine, and he gets to see all the best designs. He says, "Benford's boats all seem to have some sort of magical quality, a unique charater all their own that defies definition." And, "One often hears of a naval architect combining traditional design with modern building techniques. It may be that Jay Benford has created the ultimate marriage of the two in this breathtaking design."

You can learn more about these designs by reading *Cruising Yachts* by Jay R. Benford. It's filled with salty and practical solutions for your next cruising yacht. Use the order form and see for yourself. Only $35.00 postpaid, first class.

BENFORD 30 TRAWLER-YACHT
30' x 23'6" x 10'6" x 3'
Cold-molded, strip-planked,
Airex or steel
Many alt. interiors & rigs
Study plans $11

P.S. We Guarantee It!
If you're not satisfied that this is the greatest collection of innovative yacht designs you've seen, return the book within 15 days for a full refund.

☐ Please send Benford's *Cruising Yachts* book and Catalog Packet for the special combination price of $40.

☐ I'm already enjoying my own copy of *Cruising Yachts*. Please just send the Catalog Packet for $10.

☐ Please send me the study plans of:

_____

_____

_____

☐ Check or money order enclosed
☐ Please charge my VISA/MasterCard

Number _____

Exp. Date _____

Name _____

Address _____

_____

Phone _____

JAY R. BENFORD
P.O. Box 447–A, St. Michaels, MD 21663
(301) 745–3235

44' TRAWLER-YACHT
44' x 42' x 15'1" x 5'
Airex—easily converted to
carvel or cold-molded
Study plans $15

14' TRAWLER-YACHT "BULLHEAD"
14' x 13' x 7' x 3'
Cold-molded or Airex
2 alt. tug versions
Study plans $11

30' TRAWLER-YACHT "PETREL"
30' x 27' x 11'3" x 3'6"
Single-chine steel, plywood,
or carvel planked
Study plans $15

38' TUG-CRUISER
38' x 36' x 14' x 4'
Airex-glass
Several alt. versions
Study plans $15

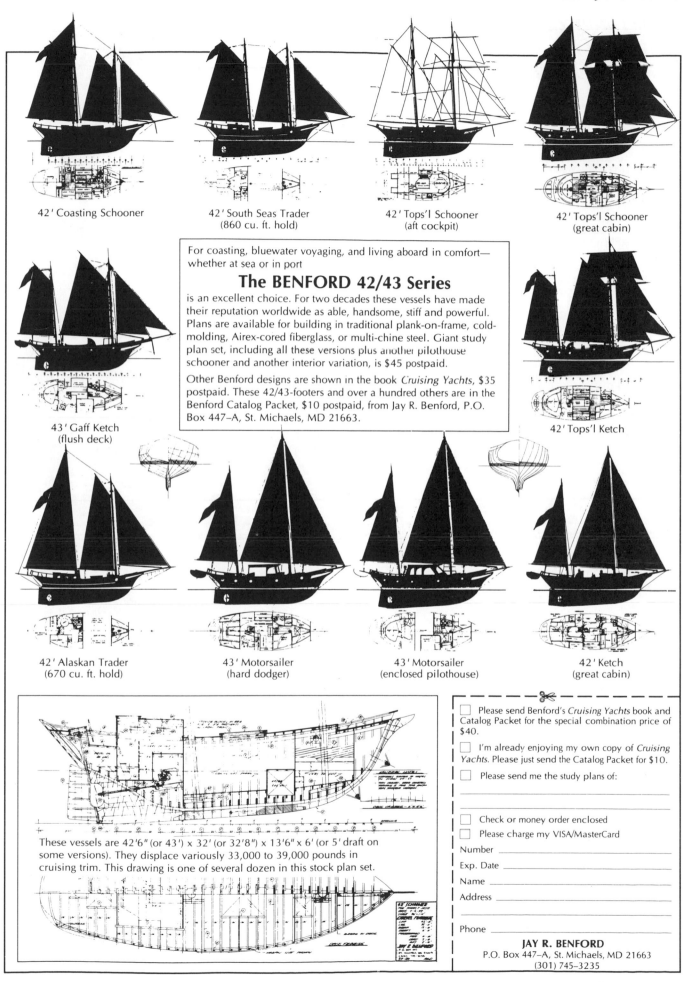

42' Coasting Schooner

42' South Seas Trader
(860 cu. ft. hold)

42' Tops'l Schooner
(aft cockpit)

42' Tops'l Schooner
(great cabin)

For coasting, bluewater voyaging, and living aboard in comfort—whether at sea or in port

The BENFORD 42/43 Series

is an excellent choice. For two decades these vessels have made their reputation worldwide as able, handsome, stiff and powerful. Plans are available for building in traditional plank-on-frame, cold-molding, Airex-cored fiberglass, or multi-chine steel. Giant study plan set, including all these versions plus another pilothouse schooner and another interior variation, is $45 postpaid.

Other Benford designs are shown in the book *Cruising Yachts*, $35 postpaid. These 42/43-footers and over a hundred others are in the Benford Catalog Packet, $10 postpaid, from Jay R. Benford, P.O. Box 447–A, St. Michaels, MD 21663.

43' Gaff Ketch
(flush deck)

42' Tops'l Ketch

42' Alaskan Trader
(670 cu. ft. hold)

43' Motorsailer
(hard dodger)

43' Motorsailer
(enclosed pilothouse)

42' Ketch
(great cabin)

These vessels are 42'6" (or 43') x 32' (or 32'8") x 13'6" x 6' (or 5' draft on some versions). They displace variously 33,000 to 39,000 pounds in cruising trim. This drawing is one of several dozen in this stock plan set.

"The magical quality of Benford's Boats"

Why did *Cruising SailboatKinetics,* "a heavily illustrated showcase of the best cruising sailboat designs of the last decade," include more designs by Jay Benford than by any other designer? The author, Danny Greene, is the design editor of Cruising World magazine and he gets to see all the best designs. He says, "Benford's boats all seem to have some sort of magical quality, a unique character all their own that defies definition." And, "Few designers are more adept at imbuing their creations with such a charming touch as Benford." And, "The most impressive feature of the Benford 38 is its enormous innovative interior and deck/cabin arrangement. Benford has the ability to combine this with a salty and charming appearance. It is hard to imagine any designer fitting more accommodations into a 30-foot waterline boat without transforming the design into a Greyhound bus." And, "As always, Benford has cleverly designed the deck and cabin to combine good appearance, spaciousness below and ease of work on deck...She will surely attract attention and compliments in any anchorage." And, "...another impeccably drawn vessel from the board of Jay R. Benford..." And, "One often hears of a naval architect combining traditional design with modern building techniques. It may be that Jay Benford has created the ultimate marriage of the two in this breathtaking design."

You can learn more about these designs by reading *Cruising Yachts* by Jay R. Benford. It's filled with salty and practical solutions for your next cruising yacht.

P.S. We Guarantee It!
If you're not satisfied that this is the greatest collection of innovative yacht designs you've seen, return the book within 15 days for a full refund.

Jay Benford is one of those freethinking designers who is just as happy working on a 14 ft. (4.27m) worldgirdler as a 131 ft. (40m) luxury cruiser. His magic is such that he can make both boats, and all those in between, individual, attractive and practical.

Cruising Yachts...is distinguished...by the chapters on Benford designs; the pages of commonsense, on design and yacht building; theory and practice of cruising and even articles on the best time to go cruising and how to get the most from your money.
Dick Johnson
Yachting World

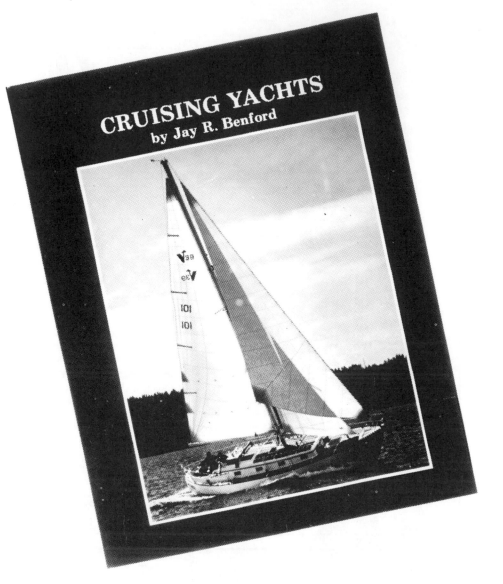

CRUISING YACHTS

by Jay R. Benford

Jay Benford is a widely known yacht designer with a far-ranging imagination and great versatility, unbound by prejudices on materials or methods of construction. This selection from his work covers both sail and power craft, from a 14-footer designed for a singlehanded circumnavigation to a 131' luxury yacht. Included are chapters on choosing a vessel, engines and horsepower, the custom design process, economy, rigs, and more. For the sailor looking for ideas, Benford is always interesting.

200 pp. Photos and study plans.
$29.95

Wooden Boat

A broad selection of Benford's inimitable cruising designs, copiously illustrated with lines, plan, profile, construction, and detail drawings, and scores of fine photographs—many in full color. Each design is discussed in detail for its concept, construction, performance, and existing and possible variations (a Benford specialty), and the book also contains articles on yacht design aesthetics, the proper offshore yacht, designing for fuel economy, the custom design process, and more. Designs include the versatile Benford 30, fully illustrated in many of its variant forms; Benford's 30' to 37½' sailing dories, "the most economical offshore cruisers"; a number of distinguished and proven cruisers in the 30' to 45' range; a 14-footer designed for singlehanded circumnavigation; several versions of the "Friday Harbor Ferry", a stable, economical, cruising houseboat that Benford believes is the shape of waterfront living to come—and well may be; and a 131' cold-molded luxury cruising yacht designed and engineers for a Brasilian client. "Magical...a unique character all their own" writes Danny Greene of Benford's designs.

Waterlines